DARK CLOUDS
SILVER LININGS

DARK
CLOUDS

SILVER
LININGS

DR. ARCHIBALD D. HART

PUBLISHING

Colorado Springs, Colorado

DARK CLOUDS, SILVER LININGS
copyright © 1993 by Archibald D. Hart, Ph.D.

Hart, Archibald D.
    Dark Clouds, Silver Linings: depression can be a healing emotion if we
learn how to cooperate with it / Archibald D. Hart.
        p. cm.
    ISBN 1-56179-091-5
1. Depressed persons—Religious life. 2. Depression, Mental—Religious
aspects—Christianity. 3. Depression, Mental—Case studies. 4. Christian
Life—1960- I. Title
BV4910.34.H37 1993
158'.1—dc20   92-33584
                                                               CIP

Published by Focus on the Family Publishing, Colorado Springs, Colorado 80995.

Distributed by Word Books, Dallas, Texas.

Unless otherwise noted, Scripture quotations are from the Holy Bible, New International
Version, copyright © 1973, 1978, 1984 by the International Bible Society.

People's names and certain details of case studies mentioned in this book have been
changed to protect the privacy of the individuals involved. However, the author has
attempted to convey the essence of the experience and the underlying principles as accurately as possible.

Some of the material in this book was previously published in Dr. Hart's book *Depression:
Coping and Caring*, which is now out of print.

Editors: Larry K. Weeden
            Joanne Sekowsky
Designer: Jeff Stoddard

Printed in the United States of America

93 94 95 96 97 98/ 10 9 8 7 6 5 4 3 2 1

CONTENTS

ACKNOWLEDGMENTS

I am deeply indebted to Dr. Carl Tracie, who helped me to compile the questions in this book. He also secured and edited the stories in section III that contribute a personal touch to the suggestions I present. While I have reworked the material substantially since it was first published, I am still thankful for Dr. Tracie's immense contribution and his continued friendship over many years.

I am also indebted to Paul Schultheis, who published the original work, for his permission to use the material from that book. I know it is his prayer that this material continue to bless God's people.

Finally, I am indebted to Nova Hutchins, my secretary, for her immense assistance in bringing this project to completion. Her untiring service to God is a great ministry to me.

Archibald D. Hart

Acknowledgments

Introduction

Depression is epidemic. One of every 18 adults—about 10 million of us—suffers from depression, a problem that seems to be on the rise. The frantic pace of life in our society, combined with a breakdown of traditional values, is taking its toll. Life is too uncertain, and its many disappointments create an appalling sense of loss. Many of our losses are tangible, such as jobs and friends. More significant are our abstract losses of security, personal worth, and control. As a culture, we may well have entered our own emotional "Great Depression."

The economic cost of being depressed in the United States is estimated in excess of $16 billion a year. Estimating the emotional and human costs of serious depression both in the lives of those suffering and in the lives of the millions more family members and friends who are affected is impossible. Those lives are often disrupted to such an extent that families disintegrate, and many have their lives turned topsy-turvy.

In the past, depression was always associated with a major mental breakdown and seemed to be restricted to a few poorly adjusted, usually anonymous, persons.

Now it has assumed a real, familiar, and very personal identity. It is found with frightening regularity in ourselves, our relatives, and our friends.

Depression is no respecter of age, sex, or occupation. We are seeing an alarming increase in childhood depression. In fact, both the "youthfulization" and aging of depression are two of its most frightening features. No longer is it just a problem of middle or later life.

Nothing is as tough to fight as depression. For some it comes swiftly, often arriving unannounced. For others it creeps up subtly over many months. When we finally realize we are in its grasp, it has already sapped our strength to fight it and fogged our minds to understand it. It knocks us flat before we have a chance to put up a defense.

Strangely enough, only about one-third of those seriously depressed will actually seek treatment. Some don't know they can be helped. Some don't accurately label what they're feeling. Most don't seek treatment because they're too depressed and feel too helpless and hopeless to believe they can get better. Many choose to "tough it out" for months or even years rather than get treatment.

Among these untreated depressed persons are, of course, many Christians. They don't realize that with the right sort of treatment, they could probably bounce back in a matter of weeks, and many could prevent any reoccurring episodes of depression. Their failure to get help is sad.

What can you do about depression? How can you deal with it and help others deal with theirs? *Dark Clouds, Silver Linings* is designed to help you cope from a Christian perspective. In it, I unmask this foe and reveal its complex (though understandable) nature and causes. The material that follows will not only help you to survive the battle, but also to emerge a healthier and wiser warrior.

The book is divided into three major sections. In the first, I provide answers to the more general questions about depression: questions concerning its definition, nature, and causes. I have also included chapters relating to depression in women and in children and adolescents.

In the second section, I offer a systematic overview of how we can bring healing to our depressions. Chapter 9 is directed specifically to spouses or friends who want to understand and support the depressed person. This distinction is not meant to restrict the use of either part, however. Anyone who suffers will benefit by reading all the material.

In the third section, three well-known people describe their experiences with depression and show how, with God's help, they arrived at healing. Joni Eareckson

Tada battled with depression as a result of an injury that left her permanently paralyzed from the shoulders down. Florence Littauer's depression resulted from the birth of two hopelessly brain-damaged children. Ministers become depressed, too, and Ben Patterson's account illustrates how fatigue, tension, and illness can paralyze even a successful Christian minister through depression. You will be encouraged by the way God, in very practical ways, used depression to teach and strengthen each of these people and to prepare them for a more effective ministry to others.

A thoughtful and prayerful reading of this material will not only help you understand depression better, but it should help you understand yourself as well. God provides us all with spiritual resources for coping with depression. To use these resources effectively, we need to understand ourselves and how our minds and bodies function. It is my prayer that you will be a more effective and understanding counselor and friend to depressed people around you. But above all, I pray you will come to understand that growth through the trauma of depression can only be fully accomplished in the context of faith and trust in Jesus Christ.

Section I

Questions and Answers about Depression

If you're an average person, you will experience a significant depression at least once in your lifetime. Typically, you'll respond in one of two ways: you will indulge it, wallowing in helplessness and self-pity; or, gritting your spiritual and emotional teeth, you will fight it with all your willpower.

The first approach will almost certainly assure a more lengthy bout with depression than is necessary. The second will likely guarantee a buildup of guilt and frustration that shows itself in one of two ways: in increasingly intense depressions or in the development of a variety of physical ailments—such as high blood pressure, ulcers, or trouble with "nerves"—that may seem to have no recognizable origin.

In many instances, you won't even realize your problem is depression. That's the nature of depression. It eludes recognition.

You may also have relatives or friends who are prone to depression. Part of you is afraid of their melancholy. You don't know what to make of it. You would like to be able to help them, but you don't know what to say or do. In fact, if you are really honest, you have to admit you're somewhat afraid of what is going on. After all, they're not acting at all like their normal selves. Should you sympathize with them or try to snap them out of their low mood with some firm talk? More than likely, you're afraid that anything you say or do will be wrong and will only cause more damage. Yet if you do nothing, aren't you likely to prolong their depression?

If you're wrestling with depression yourself, section I will help you develop a more accurate understanding of its nature and purpose. You will learn that depression is part of a warning system, a normal response to events in your life that points to values and attitudes needing attention. You'll learn to recognize the symptoms of depression in their early stages, what causes depression, and how depression is treated.

O N E

Depression:

Its Nature and Symptoms

Let's begin by exploring the nature of depression. What is it? What does it feel like? What are its symptoms? If you're like many people, you may not recognize your own depression and so may need the help of someone else to understand your situation. If you do recognize it, you may regard it as an unnatural condition, an indication of failure or weakness.

The questions and answers given here are intended to provide you with an accurate understanding of depression and to correct mistaken notions you may have about this widespread condition.

WHAT IS DEPRESSION?

Depression is the most complicated of all our emotions and yet one of the most common psychological problems a person can experience. Someone has called it the "common cold" of the emotions.

It's a feeling of gloom or sadness that is usually accompanied by a slowing down of the body. It is not just in the mind but is experienced throughout the whole body. It's in the stomach as much as in the head.

We are *all* designed to experience depression. At some time in their lives, probably two of every ten people will experience depression seriously enough to hinder their normal way of life.

WHAT IS THE NATURE OF DEPRESSION?

Depression can be seen as a symptom, a disease, or a reaction. As a symptom, depression is part of the body's warning system, calling attention to something that's wrong. It alerts us to the fact that there has been a violation of some sort. Something is missing or lost. It can also be a symptom of something physically wrong. Depression accompanies a wide variety of physical disorders, such as influenza, cancer, and certain disturbances of our endocrine system.

But depression is also a disease in itself. In its most severe form, the psychotic depressions, it is an illness category all of its own. Known as a *major depression*, it has two forms: unipolar depression (one just gets severely depressed) and bipolar depression (alternating manic and depressed moods).

Finally, depression can be a reaction to what is going on in life, or more specifically, to significant losses one experiences. This last form is known as *reactive depression*. It's the kind most people have to contend with in their daily lives. If we are emotionally healthy, we deal with those losses promptly, and the depression is short-lived. If we're not, the depression lingers and may even get worse or chronic.

ARE THERE DIFFERENT CATEGORIES OF DEPRESSION?

Broadly speaking, there are three major categories of depression. First, there are *endogenous depressions*. These come from within the body. They are generally understood to be caused by biochemical disturbances in the brain, the hormonal system, or the nervous system. Some are the direct consequence of disease or infection. We don't fully understand everything about how the brain's chemistry can be disturbed, but these depressions respond so well to antidepressant medication that it's generally accepted that they have a biochemical basis.

These depressions often occur in a cyclical manner. Every now and again the person becomes depressed, and there seems to be no reason for it. Such depressions are aggravated by fatigue and stress.

Psychotic depressions are the severest form of endogenous depression. They have nothing to do with personality and can overtake even a cheerful and upbeat person. They're called *psychotic* because the symptoms are extremely severe. Often there are delusions of hopelessness and wickedness so bizarre that it's evident the person is out of touch with reality.

The second group of depressions is known as *exogenous depressions* (meaning "from without"). These are reactions to what is going on externally, the depressions we experience in day-to-day living. They are psychological in nature.

I would characterize these as a form of grief. They are reactions to loss—part of a grieving process in which we come to terms with that loss. It's a process of "letting go." It takes us into a low mood so we can resolve our experience of the loss. This is such an important category of depression that I have devoted most of chapter 2 to it.

The third group of depressions I call the *neurotic depressions*. These differ from reactive depressions in that they're responses to the stresses and anxieties of life that have built up over a long period. They happen when we don't grieve our losses in a healthy way. Rather than coming to terms with them, we develop a lifestyle of self-pity. We begin to wallow in feeling down and sad. We retreat into depression as a way of escaping from anxiety.

Clearly, neurotic depression is unhealthy. It feeds on its own misery. A person suffering from it refuses to get out of bed and engage life. There's a pervasive sense of fear, and the depressive feelings are an escape from life. These depressions, therefore, are chronic and can easily develop into life-long patterns. They are also the most difficult to treat, especially if the sufferer doesn't want to be helped.

As we proceed, the differences between the kinds of depression will become clearer.

WHY IS DEPRESSION SO HARD TO DIAGNOSE?

Because depression can mimic many illnesses, it can often go undiagnosed for a long time. The many illnesses it can mimic include general health problems, central nervous system disturbances, gastric problems, muscular problems, heart problems, respiratory problems, and even skin problems. Depression can mask itself with anger, headaches, backaches, fatigue, irritability, hypersensitivity, and a whole range of disturbing sensations.

The gastro-intestinal tract (stomach and colon) is a common site for depressive symptoms. Often there is weight loss or the opposite, weight gain. Food and alcohol are common tranquilizers used to cover depression. Sometimes the symptoms are merely a lump in the throat or having difficulty swallowing.

Other symptoms that can mask depression include:

- Grinding of the teeth, with pain in the jaw muscles
- Frequent throat clearing of secretions in the back of the throat
- Intolerance to certain foods because of their texture
- Swallowing excessive air, with a resulting bloating that leads to a sensation of fullness in the stomach.

Headaches of all sorts also frequently mask depression. Often a person with depression undergoes extensive neurological testing, brain scans, spinal taps, and the like, but the underlying problem eludes the physician.

IS DEPRESSION A MENTAL ILLNESS?

Most depressions are not forms of mental illness. Only the severest should be called that. I don't really like the term, as it's not always clear at what point on the range of intensity, from mild to severe, we can say for sure that depression is a mental illness. Often depression is a biological illness. But when it is severe enough to disrupt an individual's life, preventing him or her from working and/or threatening life, it certainly would be considered a mental illness.

Most of us will suffer from "normal" depressions, and it would be inappropriate to label ourselves as mentally ill.

HOW DO GRIEF AND DEPRESSION DIFFER?

Grief is a form of reactive depression. Not all depression is grief, but there can be no grief without depression or sadness. An important distinction, though, is that in pure grief, hypothetically speaking, there is no self-blame or loss of self-esteem. In depression, however, there is a tendency to feel worthless and guilty. Seldom is grief pure, so even bereaved people feel some guilt about their departed loved ones, and they may also feel a degree of worthlessness.

WHEN DOES APPROPRIATE GRIEF BECOME AN INAPPROPRIATE DEPRESSION?

Mostly under two conditions. First, it happens when we blame ourselves for not being as loving, kind, and so on to our departed loved ones as we might have been, or when we experience guilt for things we did to them while they were alive. We then move from grieving the loss to being enmeshed in unhealthy feelings about a relationship that cannot now be repaired.

Second, grief becomes inappropriate depression when the grief process is unduly prolonged. This usually is a result of excessive feelings of guilt or self-blame.

ARE THE "BLUES" A FORM OF DEPRESSION?

Yes, although they're a minor form. For instance, the "Monday morning blues" are experienced by many people as they prepare to meet the demands of the week. For some, the blues are the low periods in their cycle of emotions that normally follow high periods of excitement. Those cycles are quite normal and are determined by our individual physiology, by the weather to some extent, by infections, and by many other circumstances. They are the body's way of regulating immune function and forcing us to rest. The blues should not alarm us. If we just cooperate with them, we'll improve our overall state of body and mind.

CAN WE BE ANXIOUS AND NOT BE DEPRESSED?

Anxiety and depression are separate emotions, but they can coexist. We can be anxious and not depressed, and we can be depressed and not anxious. When they coexist, such as in a depression with a lot of anxiety, we have a most disturbing condition called an *agitated depression*. The anxiety intensifies the depression and is very disabling.

WHAT IS THE RELATIONSHIP BETWEEN DEPRESSION AND WHAT WE COMMONLY CALL A NERVOUS BREAKDOWN?

This is a complex relationship made even more confusing by fuzzy definitions of the term *nervous breakdown*. The name is really a lay person's term used to describe many problems. It can be either a physical or a psychological problem. It's often used to describe extreme exhaustion when, due to failure of one of the body's systems, an individual is unable to continue coping with the ordinary demands of life.

But the relationship between depression and a nervous breakdown is even more complex. Sometimes depression accompanies a nervous breakdown. At other times it's the cause of a nervous breakdown. In other words, a nervous breakdown is simply a severe case of depression. A person reacts to some loss with a depression, which in turn puts him in a downward spiral until his body can no longer sustain him. This can lead to a collapse from extreme fatigue and exhaustion.

Sometimes a nervous breakdown is a psychotic disorder, like schizophrenia, which is a severe biological illness that can be treated effectively in most cases. There is no connection between schizophrenia and the depressions I am discussing here.

WHAT ARE THE EARLIEST SIGNS OF DEPRESSION?

The strange thing about depression is that we often can't recognize it in its early stages. We only become aware of it when it's fully developed. One of the early danger signs, though, is finding we are going deeper and deeper into depression. This intensification should alert us to the fact that something is wrong. We can't shake off the feeling, and it slowly gets worse.

IS IT POSSIBLE TO BE DEPRESSED AND NOT KNOW IT?

Yes, very much so. In fact, it's common. Depression eludes recognition. It seems to dampen our awareness of our feelings. Not only that, but the low mood, the sadness we normally associate with depression, is often a very minor aspect of depression. It's quite possible for people not to realize they're depressed when the sadness component is missing and all they feel is lethargy and lack of interest.

HOW CAN I TELL IF I'M DEPRESSED?

Most people with depression don't get appropriate treatment because they don't recognize their symptoms. They often misdiagnose their condition and seek the wrong remedy. Because depression makes you feel less valuable as a person, it's quite common to spiritualize a depression and blame it all on Satan. That's not helpful.

WHAT, THEN, ARE THE COMMON SYMPTOMS OF DEPRESSION?

- Persistent sadness, anxiety, or an "empty" mood
- Feelings of hopelessness and pessimism
- Feelings of guilt, worthlessness, helplessness (Depressed people may burst out crying for the slightest reason.)
- Loss of interest or pleasure in ordinary activities, including sex
- Sleep disturbances such as insomnia, early morning waking, or oversleeping
- Eating disturbances (either loss of weight or gain in appetite and weight)
- Decreased energy, fatigue, being slowed down
- Thoughts of death or suicide and even suicide attempts
- Restlessness and irritability
- Difficulty in concentrating, in remembering, and in making decisions
- Physical symptoms such as headaches, digestive disorders, and chronic pain that does not respond to treatment

In nearly all depression there is a state of fatigue. That's one of the essential symptoms. There's also a general lack of interest in life and of energy to perform usual duties or to engage in normal activities. The sufferer becomes lethargic, lying around a lot, refusing to get out of bed, or escaping into television watching or activities that make no demands.

ARE THERE SPIRITUAL SYMPTOMS OF DEPRESSION?

Yes, there are, and they are just as important as the physical and psychological ones. Spiritual symptoms can take two extremes:

1. The most common is to pull away from God—to feel He is rejecting us. This reaction is triggered by the excessive psychological guilt one experiences in depression. Since we feel guilty, we assume God is punishing us by rejecting us. That irrational idea leads to an actual spiritual withdrawal on our part. We neglect the Bible. We neglect to pray. We don't show interest in anything spiritual. This is unfortunate, because in so doing we turn away from the very resources that could help us. Depressed people may need to be constantly reassured that God is not rejecting them and that He is there to comfort and help.

2. The opposite reaction is to become overinvolved in spiritual things. As a desperate attempt to regain normality or cope with the depression, a person may become fanatical about religious things. This is a compensation for feelings of guilt. We spend many hours a day in prayer, not for prayer's sake, but to appease our conscience. We won't leave the Bible alone. We cling to it like a fetish. I have known some depressed people to spend five, six, or even seven hours a day in prayer and "Bible clutching" in their desperation.

Unfortunately, this overinvolvement is not always healthy. People actually become incapacitated by the preoccupation with spiritual things. It becomes a ritual and has no real meaning. Fortunately, God understands what's happening and accepts it for what it is. We have a very patient God who is not offended by our misuse of His resources. He may even turn this to our advantage; we can't always understand His ways.

IS LACK OF CONCENTRATION LIKELY TO BE RELATED TO AN UNRECOGNIZED DEPRESSION?

Depression can cause problems with concentration and other mental activities. Since depression serves to remove us from our environment, we can become preoccupied with our own thoughts and not pay attention to what's going on around us. I would emphasize, though, that a lack of concentration is more frequently caused by bad habits. Some people just don't pay sufficient attention. They're easily distracted. Anxiety can also interfere with concentration. When we're worried, we can't focus our attention on what we're doing.

What is the sequence of events when a person becomes depressed?

Perhaps the best way to understand what goes on in depression is to separate what goes on in our bodies from what goes on in our minds, although when we talk about emotions or feelings, we really refer to the combination of both.

In reactive depression, our thinking is first affected. We perceive some sort of loss. We think about it (if only for a few seconds) and realize something is now missing from our lives. Perhaps we've lost a job. Maybe we've been criticized or have even lost hope.

This thinking is paralleled by certain alterations in the body. We don't understand exactly what subtle biochemical changes accompany our thinking, but I believe they're designed by God to slow us down, to remove us from our environment by making us disinterested in normal activities, so we can deal with the loss.

The combination of these processes (psychological and physical) is what makes up the feeling of depression. We become sad and lethargic. But there are also exchanges between these two elements. Certain sensations we feel because of the way biochemical changes are evaluated in our thinking. We may not like those feelings, so they arouse other feelings (such as anger or disappointment), and those emotions, in turn, affect the way our bodies react. Thus, the cycle continues. We become sad, angry, and disappointed, and our self-esteem is diminished.

This is why we speak of our "complex" emotions. Each change causes other changes in both mind and body, which interact to keep the cycle of emotion going. Eventually, when we get our thinking under control, we can stop this negative pattern. But any biochemical change that has started will take time to settle down. A process of readjustment must take place before the body's biochemistry is restored to normal levels.

That's why it's so important to allow ourselves time to let our bodies adjust after we've corrected the thinking component of our depression. We will still feel depressed because the body's chemistry is altered. Only after the body has caught up with the mind will we feel normal again.

Are there well-defined stages of depression?

Depression is a continuum of feelings. It goes all the way from mild sadness to severe dejection. It ranges from minor blues all the way through to the most severe form of mental illness. But that doesn't mean we go from one level to another. It's wrong for people to fear they're going to end up with severe depression just because they've started to feel a little down. There are big jumps between the various levels of depression. The difference between a minor reactive depression and a severe psychotic depression, for example, is enormous.

There's no connection between the two. There are identifiable stages in a reactive depression, however. It begins with an early stage where we are busy thinking about and analyzing whatever it is we've experienced as a loss. As we start this grieving process, we find ourselves moving much deeper into depression as the implications of the loss become more apparent. Finally, however, we "bottom out" and begin to put things into perspective as we come to terms with the loss. This is the recovery phase.

We can't really speak of stages in the severe forms of depression. They come on suddenly and can deeply intensify in a matter of days. But they also stop rather suddenly, especially if they have been effectively treated.

HOW CAN WE IDENTIFY THE INTENSITY OF A DEPRESSION?

It's helpful to classify the intensity of a depression into the following categories:

1. Light depression: characterized by a low mood or a minor or temporary loss of interest in our environment, together with some feeling of discouragement. Usually our thinking isn't disturbed and remains rational. Physically, we experience a knot in the pit of the stomach. Our eating and sleeping habits remain fairly normal. Spiritually, we may engage in some temporary spiritual withdrawal, but it's not significant. We seem able to ride it out spiritually.

2. Medium depression: the symptoms just mentioned are intensified, but the feeling of hopelessness is much more dominant. There may be some crying, and thinking is now somewhat painful and slow. As we become more preoccupied with ourselves, the depression seems to dominate our lives. Some self-blame emerges. There may be some appetite loss. It may be difficult to get to sleep, but once asleep, we usually survive the night. We're not really incapacitated in any way. Spiritually, there's a tendency to pull away from God. We don't pray, and we refuse to go to church or other fellowship meetings.

3. Severe depression: everything already described occurs but is intensified. There's extreme sadness, low mood, dejection with frequent crying, extreme discouragement, and much guilt, self-blame, and self-pity. Physically, there's a severe disruption of appetite and sleep, with extremes of excess or privation. We fail to cope with our environment and begin to neglect ourselves and our appearance. We don't want to wash or change clothes. We don't want to shave or put on makeup.

We find it extremely difficult to go about our regular duties. Spiritually, we totally withdraw from all activities, or we become intensely preoccupied with religious matters.

In this brief outline, you can see that a depressed person can move from one level of depression to another. The differences are more in degree than in kind.

IS DEPRESSION A CAUSE OR A CONSEQUENCE OF LOW SELF-ESTEEM?

It can be either. If we experience a significant failure in life, the failure not only causes depression, but it also robs us of any good feelings we have about ourselves. Our self-esteem is diminished, *and* we move toward self-rejection and self-hate. The loss of self-esteem then causes more depression.

On the other hand, depression itself also produces diminished self-esteem. Part of the mood of depression is a feeling of self-rejection and hate. If we're depressed, therefore, we will also experience diminution of self-esteem. It isn't always easy to sort which is cause and which is consequence, and it probably doesn't matter. The point is that there's a strong connection between depression and self-hate. I'll have more to say on this subject in chapters 4 and 9.

WHAT BACKGROUND FACTORS MIGHT CREATE A TENDENCY TOWARD DEPRESSION?

The experience of separation early in life seems to be a significant factor in proneness toward depression. Children who are separated even for short periods from their parents often find they become easily depressed later in life. This is tied into feelings of insecurity, and it's my opinion that people who are insecure experience depression more frequently than those who are not.

People who have a long history of inability to relate adequately to others also find themselves depression prone. Perhaps the most significant situation creating depression proneness is growing up in a dysfunctional family. Those affected are victims of physical or sexual abuse, as well as children who suffer the breakup of their families through divorce.

WHEN SHOULD A PERSON SEEK PROFESSIONAL COUNSEL?

When people find that their depression is lasting longer than they feel comfortable about or if they find themselves deeply depressed, beginning to think of ways of escaping, avoiding family responsibilities, or even suicide, the time has come to seek professional help.

Sometimes, too, reactive depressions trigger severe biological reactions, and the grieving process is contaminated by biological disturbances. You then need professional help to sort out what's psychological and what's biological and to facilitate the recovery. If your depression is severe, therefore, talk to your pastor, or see your physician right away for a referral.

DO PEOPLE INCREASE IN NEED OF PROFESSIONAL HELP AS THEY PROGRESS FROM LIGHT TO SEVERE DEPRESSION?

Yes, very much so. As we go up the scale of intensity to the severe depressions, the greater is the need for outside help, because we're less and less able or willing to help ourselves. Light depressions are common experiences. We should all know how to deal with them. But medium-to-severe depressions need outside intervention, and the more severe they are, the more likely it is that the helper should be a professional.

AT WHAT POINT IS PROFESSIONAL HELP ESSENTIAL?

With the onset of a medium-intensity depression, the help that just talking to a friend can give has reached its limit. As the intensity increases, the risk that depressed people will take their lives increases. There's also a greater likelihood of a biological depression. When people begin to cry often and feel their situation is hopeless, they definitely need professional help.

IS THERE A DANGER THAT A DEPRESSED PERSON WILL ATTEMPT SUICIDE?

Suicidal thoughts don't appear until at least the medium intensity of depression is experienced. Light depressions often move us to use our resources more effectively and to cope with our situation. In that sense, they can be healthy. If we've lost our job, for example, we go out and find another so as to relieve the depression.

But in a medium-intensity depression, we begin to feel some helplessness and think about how nice it would be to escape all our troubles. Those thoughts incapacitate us, and we might even begin to think about ending life.

In severe depressions, people become totally preoccupied with escape and death wishes. Let me emphasize again that having suicidal thoughts does not mean a person is planning suicide. However, we must assume there is a high risk and take steps to deal with such thoughts. An estimated 15 percent of depressed people will ultimately take their lives.

WHAT ARE THE CLUES TO A SUICIDAL DEPRESSION?

Let me answer in two parts. First, certain conditions must exist before suicide is a possibility. One is that the depression is a consequence of a severe loss, one that cannot be replaced. (See chapter 2.) It's true that in some of the endogenous forms of depression, the biochemical disturbance producing the depression also creates a desire to escape. But most suicides occur as a result of a significant, irreplaceable loss.

Second, there is usually intense anger at the loss or at someone responsible for it. When those two conditions are combined, there is a high risk of suicide.

WHY DO DEPRESSIONS SOMETIMES OCCUR IN CYCLES?

This goes back to what I said about the cyclical nature of our emotions. They are heavily dependent on our bodies, and our bodies go through high and low cycles. Those cycles are often caused by changes in hormones or in immune system fluctuation. During the high points, it is remarkable how easily we're able to cope with life, and we seldom experience depression. During the low times, just the slightest loss can put us into a depression. We need some understanding of how our bodies operate so we can allow for those low periods. We shouldn't expect so much of ourselves during those times but should let our systems recover. If each of us did this, we could avoid much depression.

IS THERE SUCH A THING AS A BIORHYTHM, THEN?

Absolutely not in the way the concept is presented in some literature or in New Age teaching. The idea that certain physical, emotional, and intellectual cycles can be computed from your birth date is too simplistic. There are fluctuations, but they are not determined by when you were born.

We know normal physiological fluctuations do occur. Even the weather affects them. The most obvious one is the menstrual cycle in women. But even it doesn't operate with absolute regularity. Menstruation is influenced by illness, stress, and many other factors. (See chapter 3.) To try to predict any physical, emotional, or intellectual state on the basis of fixed cycles is nonsense.

WHAT IS THE DIFFERENCE BETWEEN BIORHYTHM AND BIOFEEDBACK?

The two are not the same. Biofeedback is a highly scientific technique (unlike biorhythms) using sensitive instruments to monitor physiological changes such as muscle tension, skin temperature, blood pressure, heart rate, and so on. This information is then fed back to the individual to help him or her learn how to control those bodily functions. Basically, it's a technique for teaching deep relaxation as a way of coping with or reducing stress. Biofeedback clinics help to treat headaches, painful menstruation, high blood pressure, and a host of other stress disorders.

ARE THE SYMPTOMS OF DEPRESSION DIFFERENT IN WOMEN AND MEN?

Basically, the symptoms are the same. The causes, however, may be different. There may also be slight differences in the way the sexes experience depression. Women are clearly more prone to depression. (See chapter 3.)

IS DEPRESSION RELATED TO SOCIOECONOMIC VARIABLES?

To some extent, reactive depression ought to be tied to poverty, yet the lower socioeconomic groups seem to be less prone to it. They face loss as a reality every day and so are better able to cope with life and its losses than more-affluent groups. The middle and upper classes, on the other hand, are much more prone to depression because they have so much more to lose and because their values are so much more materialistic.

Endogenous depressions, of course, play no favorites. They occur with much the same frequency right across the socioeconomic spectrum, as they're biological and even genetic in nature.

ARE UNSUCCESSFUL PEOPLE MORE LIKELY TO SUFFER DEPRESSION THAN SUCCESSFUL PEOPLE?

Very much so. The experience of failure is a significant loss in our culture. We worship success and don't know how to receive failure gracefully. That sets us up for one depression after another. It also leads to a depressive life-style where one learns to cope with life's disappointments through depression. In fact, some psychologists have tried to develop a formula by which they can predict depression proneness based on the ratio of success to failure in a person's life. The greater the experience of failure, the greater is the frequency of depression.

ARE SOME TEMPERAMENTS MORE SUSCEPTIBLE TO DEPRESSION THAN OTHERS?

Yes, depression proneness is often related to personality. The combination of inherited factors and the effect of environment can develop a particular personality that is depression prone. Such a person has an exaggerated reaction to loss and views life negatively. He or she almost searches for opportunities for self-pity and pessimism.

Do we have any choice in becoming depressed?

Sometimes we do; sometimes we don't. We have a degree of choice in how we set ourselves up for life and in the values we adopt. In that sense, we determine whether we become depressed. Even at the point of experiencing a loss, we often have a choice. We can choose to allow our depression to continue. But sometimes we're able to avoid the depression that would otherwise inevitably follow by developing our understanding of what God values and appreciating His perspective on our lives.

To put it another way, many of our minor depressions arise because we fail to see things as God does. We exaggerate our losses and make catastrophes of our failures.

Do some people subconsciously want to be depressed?

Yes, very much so. Some people have experienced depression for such a long time that it has become a life-style, a way of coping with their problems and anxieties—even with all of life. At the slightest hint of trouble, they immediately retreat into depression. In that sense, they unconsciously want to be depressed.

Is depression habit forming?

For those who develop a depressive life-style, depression becomes a habit in the sense that they use it to escape from life's realities. Their body's chemistry may become adapted to a depressed state to such a degree that it demands depression as a condition to keep the body comfortable. It then becomes difficult for them to give it up even when there is no longer any psychological or physical need to be depressed.

Will a severe depression leave a person a psychological cripple, unable to deal with life's circumstances in an ordinary way?

Not really, and certainly not if the depression is handled properly. Even the severest form of depression—the psychotic depression or manic-depressive psychosis (now called *bipolar affective disorder*)—is time-limited and will pass and leave no crippling effects whatsoever. Only when people develop a depressive and neurotic life-style over a long period is their ability to cope with life impaired. We need not be afraid of those severe depressions. As we will see, they can be treated effectively in most cases.

CAN DEPRESSION SOMETIMES BE A HEALTHY RESPONSE TO CIRCUMSTANCES?

Yes. If we can learn to cooperate with it, depression can be a healthy response, even a healing emotion. The positive side can be seen in two of its functions: it alerts us to a loss, and it helps us to detach from the lost object in a process of "letting go." These are normal and necessary steps.

Perhaps the best example I can give of this is in the experience of bereavement. A lot of evidence shows that the emotion of grief following bereavement (or the loss of a job, etc.) must be allowed full expression for healing to occur. The more freedom we give ourselves to grieve (become sad, etc.), the more rapid is our recovery from the grief. We speed up the "letting go."

Depression can also be a positive factor in the physical realm. It is a symptom of many illnesses, including the flu. The depression helps the healing by detaching us from activity. If we didn't detach and slow down, the illness could kill us. So our sadness and loss of interest in normal activities aids the healing process.

I believe depression is designed by God to warn us that we're getting into deep water, to slow us down, to remove us from the business of life, and to pull us back so we can pay attention to what's happening. I would even say it's designed to drive us back to God, to turn our trust to Him and find resources for help.

IS THERE A DIFFERENCE BETWEEN SPIRITUAL AND PSYCHOLOGICAL DEPRESSION?

Yes, there are important differences, and we need to clarify them.

Spiritual depression has to do with the deep feeling of discontent or dissatisfaction with one's life that we feel when we're out of touch with God. This feeling may be focused sharply by breaking one of God's laws, or it may be a more general feeling brought on by living under a wrong set of values. In either case, this type of depression results from a loss of the awareness of God, or a loss of being comfortable with Him. In other words, spiritual depression is what we feel when alienated from God. There may be psychological components, but it is more a spiritual than a psychological experience.

True psychological depression has to do with just being human. It is in many respects a normal and natural response to life's losses. As such, psychological depression should not separate us from God. For many of us, however, psychological depression does alienate us from God. It may cause us to feel He has abandoned us. But nothing is further from the truth. We need to hold to our faith and believe God is always there, comforting us in our losses.

CAN YOU GIVE AN EXAMPLE OF HOW THESE DIFFER?

Spiritual and psychological depression differ in several ways, although they often commingle. Suppose we have a young man who is very ambitious. He wants rapid promotion and is prepared to do anything to get it. So he engages in a dishonest sales promotional activity. People are ripped off by being misled. Soon he finds himself trapped in a situation that he knows is clearly unethical, perhaps even illegal. The sales promotion fails, everything is brought into the open, and the young man finds himself very depressed. His reputation has been sullied. Where will he get another job?

I would call this a spiritual depression, with psychological consequences. The primary cause is the violation of principles he knows are right and which he believes he has received from God. As a result, God convicts him of his sin. He feels the loss of God. He also feels the loss of his job, so he becomes deeply depressed. He misreads God's conviction, and that complicates his depression. If he could only hear what God was really saying to him, his depression would be spiritual and far easier to deal with.

What is God's message? "I am displeased. Something is not right. I want you to put your life back on a righteous track." God is not pulling away from him to punish him. Neither has God abandoned him, though that's what he feels. Rather, God is calling him to healing. The very loss of God he's feeling is designed to point him to the real problem. He needs to hear it and take correction so the loss can be restored.

It's also most important to realize that spiritual depressions have psychological dimensions. Our young man may need some psychological help. But his is primarily a spiritual depression, and the spiritual components have to be dealt with before he can expect any healing. Sadly, this distinction is not made by secular psychotherapists.

Let me give an example of a psychological depression with no spiritual components. You're driving to work one morning when out of the blue, you're not quite sure how, you're involved in an accident. You've hit the car ahead of you, and the one behind has run into you as well. All three cars are severely damaged. You don't know whether your insurance will cover the cost or whether the accident was even your fault. Still, you feel responsible and stupid.

Very soon you're in a depression. That's natural. You've suffered a loss. You may or may not have been responsible. But accidents happen. Dogs run into roads; people are startled and jam on their brakes. Who knows why the accident occurred? You're depressed, however, and it may last several days or even weeks.

This depression has no spiritual component to it. It is purely psychological, with some biological reaction following shock. You have not alienated God or violated His principles in any way. You have just had an unfortunate accident.

The accident may cause some spiritual reaction, however. You may blame God for not protecting you. You may become angry at Him for allowing this accident to happen and so withdraw from Him. (It's the adult form of pouting.) That's unfortunate, because now you're not using God's resources to help you through the depression.

Fortunately, God understands how you feel. What you should do is accept the fact that you're experiencing a psychological depression and turn to God for help. He can assist you with the grieving process.

While spiritual and psychological depressions are different, then, the resources for healing them both are available to us through our faith in what we believe God is able to do for us. God should never be shut out of our depressions, no matter what their cause. He desires to help us get through them and to learn more about ourselves as we do.

WHY DO MANY CHRISTIANS ATTACH A STIGMA TO DEPRESSION?

Unfortunately, this stigma does exist, especially in evangelical Christian circles. It is born out of ignorance. People are afraid of what they don't understand. There are probably many reasons for this stigma, but let me suggest three.

First, in our culture we have strong expectations that people should be in control of themselves and their emotions. Depression is seen as a sign that we're out of control, so we fear it.

Second, this general fear is exaggerated in Christian circles by our emphasis on notions of "perfection." No one should be weak, we erroneously believe. Depression is seen as a failure and is therefore stigmatized.

Third, we fear that depression in its severest form is a mental illness. To some extent that's true, but it's really a physical illness, not a mental one. Only the symptoms are mental. We may feel we're on a downward path toward a severe mental illness. Such a fear is unwarranted, just as is stigmatizing depression.

WHAT DOES THE BIBLE HAVE TO SAY ABOUT DEPRESSION?

As a Christian, I find a lot of comfort in knowing from Scripture that depression has been around a long time. But the Bible helps in other ways as well. First, it's an excellent resource in coping with depression. The Psalms, for example, have been a comfort to depressed people in every age. Scripture restores our trust in God and helps us put things in perspective, a vital step in resolving depression.

The Bible also says to me that depression is the common lot of humanity, a normal reaction to life. Saints in both the Old and New Testaments experienced it. Scripture reminds me I'm only human. But it also encourages me to realize I don't always have to be depressed. If I get my values straight and develop a meaningful faith and trust in God, I can avoid a lot of depression.

IS DEPRESSION A SIN?

Not everything we believe as Christians is necessarily biblical or truthful. Some beliefs make us more prone to depression than non-Christians, and many well-meaning writers have caused a lot of unnecessary emotional pain by condemning depression as sin. Unless we have a sound biblical understanding of sin, it can cause significant depression.

However, when a person becomes a Christian, it's quite common to experience an intensified awareness of one's sinfulness. Unless that is coupled with a deep sense of God's forgiveness, it can deepen depressions associated with sin. That's a legitimate depression, a symptom that something is wrong. But it should not be the cause for further despair. Our increased awareness of sin should instead be a means of spiritual growth. Unfortunately, some Christian groups exaggerate this awareness of sin to the point that it becomes pathological. The sufferer is incapable of receiving God's forgiveness. Let me say again that all depression is *not* sin. Depression may be the *consequence* of sin, but it may also be a natural and normal reaction to loss. Not to feel those losses would be to deny our humanity.

In the case of endogenous depressions, labeling them as sin is as wrong as calling appendicitis a sin.

IS DEPRESSION CAUSED BY SIN DIFFERENT FROM THAT CAUSED BY LOSING A LOVED ONE?

Yes. When depression is caused by sin, we not only experience a loss of self-esteem and a loss of control over the events following the sin, but we also lose the peace of God in our lives. That can have a much greater effect than experiencing a loss of something legitimate, like losing a loved one. The loss of spiritual resources available to us as Christians is very significant when depression is caused by sin. So there is both a quantitive difference (intensity is greater) and a qualitative difference (the emotional pain is deeper). One might also say the loss of a loved one is likely to drive us back to God, whereas the depression caused by sin is likely to drive us away from Him.

SHOULD A CHRISTIAN FEEL GUILTY ABOUT BEING DEPRESSED?

Heaven forbid! One of the consequences of depression is increased guilt. That's why so many feel guilty when they're depressed. If the guilt gets out of control, it increases the depression, which is not healthy.

Depression should be seen as something like pain. It's a warning that alerts us that something is wrong. If the *cause* of the depression is a sinful activity or attitude (stealing or hating), we *should* feel guilty about that sin. But the guilt is not over the depression.

There's a bit of a paradox here, however. Depression itself often intensifies or exaggerates guilt feelings. If we allow the guilt feelings over the sinful activity to spread into feeling guilty about the depression itself, we can easily put ourselves into a despairing spiral in which our depression slowly intensifies and we become more and more depressed. So be very cautious about allowing yourself to feel too much guilt over your depression.

IS DEPRESSION A FAILURE TO TRUST GOD'S PROMISES?

This is another idea often suggested by well-meaning but uninformed Christian writers. Again let me say that it's not the depression itself but what leads up to it that can be a failure to trust God's promises. For example, we may not be trusting God in the area of values or security. The depression that follows is a consequence or symptom of that failure. But the depression itself is a normal and natural reaction to the failure, and it must run its course.

IF GOD LOVES US, WHY DOES HE ALLOW US TO BECOME DEPRESSED?

This question really ties into the larger question of why God allows tyranny, war, poverty, and hunger, or why we get sick or suffer. As human beings, we're designed to experience many emotions, not just joy. Sadness is also necessary.

We don't understand fully what purpose the painful emotions serve, but they do seem to drive us to God. If we were happy all the time, maybe we wouldn't feel we needed Him. Physical pain is an essential warning system; without it, we'd be killed the moment we walked out the front door, since we wouldn't know what to avoid. And in the same way, God created us with the ability to feel emotional pain so we are warned when things are emotionally dangerous.

DOES GOD PUNISH US THROUGH DEPRESSION?

God does not use depression as punishment. In fact, He has put all punishment "on hold" until His day of reckoning. He may discipline or chastise us, but He doesn't punish us while we live under grace. God's call to us is to repent. Christ died on the cross to bear our sins; He has become our punishment. That is past. It's finished.

Nevertheless, depression is often the consequence of going our own way. It's the warning that something has gone wrong. We might think of it as a form of punishment at the time, but it's more like the consequence of breaking a leg if we try to defy the law of gravity.

I see depression as a healing emotion. If we respond to its message and deal with what has gone wrong, we're the better for it. It should drive us back to God and to the resources He has made available. It should motivate us to repent and seek forgiveness. Depression, then, can be a gateway to health.

CAN DEPRESSION BE GOD'S WILL FOR ME?

Yes and no! *Yes* in the sense that God has moral laws just as He has physical laws in nature. If I jump from a high wall, I will break a leg. That is God's will as embodied in His natural law.

But *no* in the sense that God doesn't send depression to punish us or just to force us back on track. Many who become depressed for no apparent reason can turn their depression to good advantage. We can turn an endogenous depression into God's will for us if we can trust that He has some purpose in creating us and accept that what we're experiencing is His will.

IS DEPRESSION A SIGN THAT WE'VE FAILED IN LIVING ABOVE OUR CIRCUMSTANCES?

We must distinguish clearly between the major types of depression before we can answer that question. People suffering from endogenous depression cannot think about "rising above" it. Biological factors over which they have no direct control will be at work. What they need is medication for the depression and ongoing therapeutic support. To tell them to rise above the depression and master it would be like saying to a person with a broken leg, "You need to rise above your broken leg and get on with your life." What the person really needs is a doctor to set the leg so it can heal.

In certain reactive depressions, it would be equally inappropriate to speak of rising above circumstances. In bereavement, for example, we should be allowed to do our grieving thoroughly and completely. That allows us to put the loss in perspective and to let the departed loved one go.

There is one type of depression, however, where it's appropriate to call people to rise above their circumstances: namely, when they are depressed because they're not content with their lives (see Phil. 4:11). We all need to learn how to be contented.

DO CHRISTIANS SUFFER FROM DEPRESSION AS FREQUENTLY AS NON-CHRISTIANS?

In my experience, yes. Being Christian doesn't make us immune to depression. If anything, we might even become more sensitive to injustices and life's pains, so we feel with and for others who hurt. But Christians have resources available that can help them cope with life and their depressions more effectively. Unfortunately, the church hasn't adequately taught people how those resources can be applied to emotional problems such as depression. Sadly, some Christians are suspicious of any form of psychological help, even if it's offered by thoroughly evangelical psychologists. We have a long way to go before our Christianity embraces the whole person—body, mind, and spirit.

T W O

The Causes
of Depression

What causes depression? In the first chapter I talked about the three types of depression—endogenous, from within the body; exogenous, from without; and neurotic depression. In this chapter I want to consider the major causes of depression, with particular emphasis on the concept of loss and how we must all learn to deal with life's losses.

Life is full of potential for loss. From the day we're born, we begin to "lose" things. With the passage of time, we grow older and leave behind (a form of loss) the safety of our homes, parents, and secure childhoods. We launch into marriage and soon discover the loss of our independence and autonomy. When we reach the final stage of life, not only do we lose friends through death, but we also begin to become acutely aware of the loss of our own faculties and the inevitable final loss of our lives.

All of life, therefore, is full of losses, and along the way we have to learn to deal with them. If we don't, we become depression prone.

CAN YOU DESCRIBE THE KIND OF LOSSES
YOU'RE TALKING ABOUT?

Let's take a look at some of the many losses you may have experienced. Perhaps you grew up in a dysfunctional home and never really had a good childhood. That's a loss. Perhaps a friend has moved away from your hometown and now lives in some distant area. You've lost a friend. Perhaps a son or daughter has become a missionary and serves in a foreign land. While a part of you rejoices in your child's service for Christ, another part longs for the companionship of your child. That's a loss.

Perhaps you're a student, and that term project you turned in to your teacher or professor didn't earn you the expected *A*. That's a tremendous blow to your self-esteem. You might even feel a little unsure of yourself as a result. That represents even more loss.

Perhaps you're a business person who has invested in the stock market. Suddenly the market plunges, and you go from feeling fairly secure to facing financial disaster. The loss of financial security can be devastating in our world, because we depend so much on money to survive.

Perhaps you're a mother who has discovered her son is a drug addict or that her daughter's marriage is on the rocks. These are major losses. Or maybe your heart aches for your grandchildren, and your own emotions suddenly take a plunge into dark despair.

Perhaps you're a young man who has had an eye on a particular girl in your college group at church. You keep hesitating, wondering how to find the courage to ask her for a date. One day you learn she is dating another young man in the group. You've lost an opportunity to get to know her, your heart is devastated, and you go into a deep funk. For days or even weeks, you find yourself unable to concentrate or take any interest in your usual activities.

Perhaps you're an older person, and just the other day you took a good look in the mirror under a bright light. The years are beginning to show deep crevices and sagging skin, and you suddenly realize how much older you're getting. The thought doesn't please you.

Getting older is a form of loss. You have a birthday coming up, and you almost dread the day, because it will remind you once again of how quickly your life is passing.

What do all those experiences have in common? They all produce reactions of sadness, because they all represent experiences of loss, and there is little we can do to avoid most of them. We just have to muster the courage to face and accept them. The more effectively we do, the less we're likely to struggle with depression. When we don't adjust to the losses, we become depressed.

WHAT FORMS CAN LOSS TAKE?

Loss can take many forms. It can be the loss of a loved object, or it can be the loss of something as abstract as self-esteem or ambition.

Sometimes loss takes the form of separation or change. I recently counseled with a pastor's wife whose oldest daughter had just married. The mother and daughter were very close. Although the marriage was exciting, it represented a significant loss for the mother. Not only was her daughter moving away from their hometown, but she was also beginning to build her own family, becoming less dependent on her mother for support and love. It's not surprising that the mother went into a temporary deep depression.

Moving from one job to another can also represent loss. We develop relationships in our work experience, and even when there's the joy of promotion or the excitement of a new challenge in a new job, the separation from those we've worked with can represent a significant loss. It's losses of all sorts, often subtle or complex, that underlie psychological forms of depression.

EXACTLY HOW DOES LOSS CAUSE DEPRESSION?

A universal reaction is built deeply into every human mind and body that responds to loss with depression. It is automatic and natural. In fact, we also see it in various animals, though to a much lesser extent. It is the mind and body's way of coping with loss, and in that sense it's a protective mechanism. It goes into action to help us into a sort of hibernation while we deal with the loss.

In other words, depression has a purposeful function. It's designed to help us come to terms with the loss and to force us to adjust in such a way that we release the lost object.

Can you imagine what it would be like if we couldn't "let go" of what we've lost? Some people whose loved ones die are unable to bury them. They embalm them, encase them in glass, and do everything they possibly can to keep the presence of the loved one with them. That's very sad. Such people never really come to terms with the loss and end up being miserable. God's order is that we experience losses with maturity and be willing to let them go.

This purposeful nature of depression is perhaps easier understood when we talk about the loss of a loved one, but it's the same for other losses as well. It applies, for example, to being criticized by a friend or hearing your husband suddenly announce he's having an affair and wants to leave the marriage.

In many respects, all losses are similar. It's just a matter of degree, and even though some of our more-complex losses are more abstract, they are nonetheless still significant losses for the mind to cope with.

When someone criticizes us, the loss is usually a combination of the rejection we feel from that person and the loss of esteem we feel for ourselves. The criticism implies that the other person doesn't accept us totally or finds fault with us, and we tend to accept a part of every criticism as valid, so we reject ourselves as well.

All this is to say that loss can be a complex experience. It can take the form of concrete losses, like losing your wallet or purse, or it can take the form of such subtle and abstract losses as the loss of love, esteem, ambition, ideals, and various forms of disappointment and helplessness.

IS IT ALWAYS NECESSARY TO BE DEPRESSED AFTER A SIGNIFICANT LOSS?

Always. If you don't experience some depression, something is probably wrong. The depression may be slight, but it should be there. The only point at issue is its intensity. While depression as a response to loss is always legitimate, you don't have to be as deeply depressed as people often are. Many of our depressions are unnecessarily severe because we value the wrong things and don't trust God. The more we trust, the better we're able to appropriate the resources He has for us, and the less intense will be our depression.

CAN THESE LOSSES BE CATEGORIZED?

It's helpful to put our losses in one of four different categories, because that gives us a better handle on what's happening. The four basic categories are:

1. *Concrete losses:* These involve the loss of tangible objects. They include having an automobile accident, dropping and breaking a camera, or having our dog die. Life is full of such losses.

2. *Abstract losses*: These can be just as real as the first category of losses, but they're made up of intangibles like the loss of love, ambition, self-respect, or control. Many things we value are abstract in nature. Abstract losses are not always the creations of our own minds; they can achieve reality in themselves. I may not be able to see love, but I can certainly feel it.

3. *Imagined losses*: These come from our active imaginations. We can imag-

ine both concrete and abstract losses. We imagine that a friend has snubbed us or that someone dislikes us. We think people are talking about us or that we might lose a job. These imaginations set us up for loss and depression just as if the actual loss has occurred.

For instance, let's suppose you suddenly discover you have a lump somewhere in your body. It concerns you, so you want to see your doctor. But you can't get an appointment for two days because she's so busy. So for those two days your imagination goes wild. You begin to suspect that all sorts of things are wrong with you. You play out this imagination to such an extent that you create losses that are as real to your mind as concrete ones. The resultant depression is exactly the same as if you had experienced some actual loss.

Sometimes the depression we experience from imagined losses is even greater than that for real losses, because we can't set adequate boundaries. Imagination can't be contained. It goes far beyond reality and triggers depressive reactions way beyond what's reasonable.

A vivid imagination, therefore, is a serious handicap when it comes to depression. You have to be careful not to let it take over whenever you feel the threat of a loss or you anticipate some experience that has the potential for loss. Imagined losses are difficult to deal with simply because they haven't actually taken place.

We can often resolve imagined losses by testing the reality of our imaginations. Have those things actually happened? Just realizing our imaginations have been faulty can clear up the depression.

4. Threatened losses: The fourth category of losses is threatened losses. Because no actual loss has yet taken place, the grieving process cannot be completed. Imagine having an elderly parent who is on the verge of death. You start feeling depressed, and the grieving process begins, but until the actual death takes place, you can't complete it. You will continue to feel depressed as long as the threat of loss hangs over your head.

WHY ARE IMAGINED LOSSES SO EASILY CREATED?

For two reasons. First, the human mind is capable of such rich thought. It knows no limits. Second, we live in a society that doesn't communicate clearly. Both contribute to feed our imaginations.

We play lots of games with each other. We send hidden messages, and we're not honest, so we leave people guessing. Nor do we understand what others are saying. The result is that we're left to imagine all sorts of losses, and often we imagine much more than is really true. Our fertile minds can feed off the littlest things—a gesture, hint, or mistake—and turn them into big losses.

Is this true of Christians as well?

Absolutely. It's a sad fact that Christian people are not always honest with each other. Sometimes we don't want to reveal ourselves because we're afraid others will reject us, so we avoid being open. That feeds a lot of imagined losses in others.

Is "transparency" a good guard against this kind of depression?

I think so, assuming that acceptance goes along with the transparency. Generally, the more transparent we are and the more accepting we are of one another, the more we can be honest in love. That reduces a lot of imagined losses. We may experience some real loss as a consequence of this transparency, but real losses are always easier to deal with. They have clear limits, whereas imagined losses have no limits. Personally, I'd rather deal with one real loss than have to live with ten imagined losses and all the depression they could trigger!

Which category of loss is the hardest to deal with?

Threatened losses are perhaps the most serious of all and create the most-debilitating type of depression. We can't prevent the depression completely, because there is the possibility of a real loss. On the other hand, we can't complete our grieving and resolve the depression, because the loss hasn't actually occurred yet. So we're caught in a sort of "suspended" state that prolongs the depression as the threat of loss continues to hang over our lives.

What determines the intensity of a depression?

The intensity of a depression is determined very much by the significance or meaning of the loss. Sometimes a loss is relatively minor, so the sadness that follows it is mild and short-lived. Most of us probably don't even notice those minor depressions.

Not long ago, I found myself speeding down the road on my way to work.

Before I realized it, a big, black car with flashing red lights appeared in my rearview mirror, and I had to pull over. The police officer was very polite as he wrote out the traffic citation. It was no big deal. Five miles over the speed limit is hardly anything to be broken up about.

However, I did feel some humiliation, and the waste of the money I would have to cough up to pay the ticket irked me. For the rest of the day, I felt mildly down, even sad. Fortunately, by the time evening came it had passed away. Many minor depressions resolve themselves automatically like that and do not require any special attention or adjustment.

But not all losses are minor. And the more meaningful the object lost, the deeper will be the depression, and the greater will be the adjustment we have to make to accept the loss. This is why perhaps the deepest form of reactive depression follows the loss of a loved one in death.

Frequently, many minor losses can accumulate to become big ones. If on my way to work I get stopped for a minor speeding offense, I may feel a little depressed. If, after having just left the august presence of the policeman, I suddenly feel my car shaking and pull over to discover I have a flat tire, I might begin to feel even more depressed.

Now imagine that when I open the trunk, I discover my spare tire is also flat. Then I check my appointment book and realize I have a meeting starting in five minutes, and I'm still 20 minutes' drive from work. Now I have five losses. Furthermore, nobody stops to give me a ride as I stand on the side of the road with flat tire in hand. You can see how this accumulation of losses, even though each is relatively minor in itself, is beginning to create a significant reaction in me.

One of the key principles we need to learn, therefore, is not to allow our losses to accumulate. We need to deal with each loss separately or, at least, not allow self-talk to encourage them to pile up on each other. When I had the flat tire, if I had told myself this incident had nothing to do with my getting a ticket, I might have broken the connection. Discovering the spare tire was flat and that I was going to be late also needed to be kept as separate issues by healthy self-talk.

HOW DOES OUR HISTORY SENSITIZE US TO LOSS?

The tendency to accumulate smaller losses into a bigger one is often the result of having experienced many losses before. The more losses we've had earlier in life, particularly during childhood, the more likely we are to react to later losses with an exaggerated response.

I experienced several major losses when I was about 12 years old. My parents had decided to divorce, which by itself provoked some significant anger and depression. I soon discovered, as well, that my mother intended to move away from where we had been living, so there was the threat that I would also have to change schools. The thought of losing our home, my friends, and familiar play locations was devastating.

For several years following my parents' divorce, other significant losses also occurred. As a result, I became very sensitive to losses. I came to expect, almost daily, that something terrible would happen to me. With that mindset, of course, every little disappointment and every minor rejection became a big issue in my mind. One loss seemed to come on top of another, and in my young mind I wasn't able to separate them. As a result, depression came easily and often. Only later in life did I learn how to correct my thinking and stop the overreactions.

I have worked with many patients who suffered significant losses in childhood that now affect them in adult life. One young man, who admits he is not intellectual, experienced a number of failures during childhood. His father was forceful and pushed him into activities at which he was not good. He was required to take subjects at school he knew he couldn't master, and as a result of those failures he is now very sensitive to any form of defeat.

Even a simple task like changing a flat tire can be stressful for him. He always feels that if he doesn't do the job in under one minute, he's unsuccessful. He views everything through that one filter: failure. He constantly judges his every action as either a success or a defeat. Most of the time, he judges his actions as failures and so accumulates many losses. Not surprisingly, he is frequently depressed.

Losses need to be kept separate, therefore, if we're going to be emotionally healthy and build a happy life. We must also be able to receive the inevitable losses of life with grace. While the reaction of sadness is natural and inevitable, there are many things we can do to recover more quickly from our depressions. The more efficiently and speedily we come to terms with our losses, the happier we'll be.

God understands the role losses play in developing our sadnesses. Even Jesus became sad. Remember how He cried at the tomb of Lazarus. He had lost a dear friend. He cried with real tears because He felt sad about what had happened, even though He knew He could restore Lazarus to life. There are times when we may have to cry as well; crying can help us to grieve our losses.

CAN OUR ATTITUDES AND BEHAVIORS CAUSE DEPRESSION?

Very definitely. For example, examine the following list, and see how many of these issues have caused you depression in your past:

Discontentment: a tendency to envy others and be dissatisfied with what you haven't got or to resent what you have got.

A faulty set of values: misjudging what's important in life, and a tendency to focus too much on petty issues.

Faulty beliefs: a tendency to believe everything should go your way or that life should only present you with its blessings.

Faulty reactions: to be overly sensitive about what is said or done to you, or to be immature and not able to put things in proper balance.

In addition, many of life's circumstances can give rise to losses that can cause depression. These include:

Financial difficulties

We live in a money-dependent, materialistic society. Money is our symbol of value. We work for money, not food or clothing directly.

The more materialistic we are, the more likely we are to experience reactive depressions. The more we value the material things of this life, good as they may be, the more we will experience loss and therefore depression.

With the instability of the world's economy, more and more people have less and less to survive with. That represents significant losses and can be a major cause of depression.

Problems at work

Since we all have to earn our keep, relationships in the workplace become a major source of tension and disruption. We have to learn how to work in increasingly crowded conditions, as well as how to relate to many people we would not normally count as our friends. These problems can be a significant cause of depression.

Problems with family and children

Those closest to us are often the cause of our deepest pain. Parents whose children aren't turning out quite the way they wanted can experience significant losses. And in almost every household, there's conflict over discipline. Sometimes this conflict is between parents, but more often it's between parents and children. This is a serious source of depression.

Problems with habits

Many become addicted to certain behaviors and develop habits that can be a source of depression. Addictions such as smoking, alcohol, and drugs can cause serious biological disturbances, and they can be the source of other trouble as well, including family discord and marital breakup. People who get hooked on thrilling or exciting behaviors have their letdowns eventually. Even workaholics can find themselves prone to depression.

Low self-esteem

For many, low self-esteem is both the source of depression and a symptom of it. As I said before, low self-esteem can cause you to become depressed, but it can also be the consequence of your depression.

Growing old

For many of us, growing old will be a traumatic experience. When we're young, we hardly ever think about death and dying. But as we get to the middle and then into the final stages of life, the realization that we have only a limited life span becomes very real. It's at these times that both men and women start to think about what they haven't achieved or what is still left to be done. That can be the source of significant depression.

Loneliness and boredom

We have increasingly become a lonely society. The more we're crowded together in our cities, the more likely we are to be isolated in our little cubicles, cut off from other people. I know many large churches where people feel lonely and isolated despite being surrounded by so many other worshipers.

Loneliness and boredom, therefore, can be serious causes of depression. If you don't have a clear sense of God's purpose in your life to help overcome such depression, or if you don't have a clear sense of how God is working to make you the sort of person He wants you to be, loneliness and boredom can be overwhelming.

On this last point, many studies have shown that the sharp rise in the incidence of depression since World War II is largely the result of our society's loss of hope and faith, along with a decline in commitment to religion, the family, the nation, and the community. As modern society abandons traditional values we have held dear as Christians, we can expect a further increase in depression. The modern person is confused, lonely, abandoned, and despairing. Those are all significant causes for depression.

Unconnectedness

People without connections to family, church, and meaningful existence will struggle to find purpose in their lives and will experience more depression. One necessary condition for meaning is to be attached to something larger than yourself. People who don't take their relationship to God seriously lack the chief resource for coping with life's problems and losses. People who aren't connected to a family or find no meaning in their lives will be at even greater risk for depression.

This means, then, that as Christians we have a unique resource for helping people cope with depression. We also have a great missionary and evangelistic opportunity right where we live.

HOW DOES DISAPPOINTMENT WITH PERSONAL PERFORMANCE RELATE TO DEPRESSION?

In our culture, where we prize success and performance so much, anything that smacks of failure is a blow to our self-esteem and is going to lead to depression. Failure represents a deep sense of personal loss, more so than the loss of material things. It's probably the largest single cause of loss leading to depression, and it's also the basis for the deepest forms of reactive depressions.

IS THE SO-CALLED MID-LIFE CRISIS A CAUSE OF DEPRESSION?

Many mid-life crises, especially in men, are triggered by depression, but the situation is much more complex than that. A mid-life crisis is both a *cause* and a *consequence* of depression.

Let me illustrate the latter first, because people often don't realize that mid-life crises can be precipitated by a depression. Suppose a man reaches the middle of his life and realizes things are not going well. He is failing at his job. He hasn't accomplished his goals, and his ambitions are beginning to fade. He also realizes he's getting older, that youth and opportunity are passing him by. He experiences these as losses and becomes depressed.

This depression can lead to a crisis where he frantically and impulsively tries to replace some of his losses. He looks at his marriage and says, "The first thing I should do is to find another wife. If I were married to someone else, I'm sure I would be able to accomplish my goals." So he abandons his marriage and goes off with another, usually younger, woman. Thus, the depression he felt over job failure led to a larger crisis and started a series of events designed to relieve the depression.

But a mid-life crisis can also be the cause of depression. A woman in her mid-forties goes to work for the first time. Her children are off her hands, and she wants to do something meaningful with her life. But as she builds a career, she begins to think she has missed out on life. She starts to "live it up," has several affairs, and then suddenly comes to her senses. But now she's depressed. She feels stupid and ashamed at having lost her head. Her crisis is over, but not her depression.

It's best, perhaps, to see mid-life crisis and depression as being bound up together interdependently.

CAN DEPRESSION COME "OUT OF THE BLUE," SO TO SPEAK, FOR NO APPARENT REASON?

Depression may seem to come out of the blue, but there is always a cause, either physical or psychological. The problem is that we can't always identify the reason. We don't yet understand the complexity of the body or mind. When a person becomes fatigued, for example, depression can seemingly come from nowhere, but of course it's the result of the fatigue. The body is not able to sustain the person in coping with life. This might be mystifying to the individual. Some endogenous depressions may apparently come on quite suddenly, but here again, there's a real cause for the depression.

WHAT ABOUT DEPRESSIONS THAT COME FROM OUR EXPERIENCES?

Depression arising from past experiences also seems to appear out of the blue. But again, there's always a reason for a depression, even if it's not clear at the time.

Many of us have unfinished business from our pasts: unhappy homes, abusive parents, disappointments, and failures. They have not been resolved and may at some time or another emerge as depressions whenever we sense the losses associated with them. When that happens, we may need to do some grieving all over again.

AREN'T SUDDEN DEPRESSIONS FRUSTRATING TO DEAL WITH?

Yes, they are. Because they come on suddenly and without apparent reason, they increase our frustration—and our reaction may add further depression.

Unable to see an immediate explanation, we begin to look for reasons. It's common for people to blame their spouses, their children, their parents, or their jobs. A number of my clients have come to me with long lists of "causes" for their depressions. "Well, it's because my husband never talks." "It's because my wife isn't affectionate." "It's because my parents never loved me enough." They all sound plausible, but little of it can be proved.

Such thinking doesn't do much good, because it externalizes the blame for the depression when the people should be looking inwardly for the cause. We must remember that others don't cause us to become depressed. We allow ourselves to be depressed. And we're the only ones who can unlock the prison door to let us out of our depression. Many circumstances from our past and present can't be changed. The healthiest thing to do is to grieve the losses connected with those circumstances and get on with our lives.

CAN WE THINK OURSELVES INTO A DEPRESSION?

All reactive depressions are a result of thought processes. They arise because we *perceive* something as loss. That means we think, reason, and process the loss. It's not the loss per se that makes us depressed but our perception of it and the thinking we engage in after we perceive it. If we've been robbed, we probably won't experience depression until we arrive home and get over the shock. At that point our thinking will be focused on our fear and losses, and the depression will be triggered.

But we don't need an actual traumatic event to start the process. We can literally think ourselves into depression by dwelling on little reflections of minor events and interpreting them as catastrophic.

That's why I am strongly convinced that the best way to minimize depression is to modify our thinking — to learn to think clearly and rationally.

HOW DO OUR "ATTACHMENTS" RELATE TO LOSS?

To understand reactive depression, not only must we understand the concept of loss and see how we're created to respond with a grieving process, but we also need to understand the idea of "attachment." The greater our attachment to someone or something, and the more tightly we hold on, the greater will be the experience of depression.

We form many attachments in life. A mother gives birth to a child, and immediately a bond occurs that is a form of attachment. The young father who sees the baby for the first time also undergoes a remarkable attachment. I remember this experience clearly when each of our three girls was born. It was as if from that moment onward they were a permanent part of me.

When we develop friendships, we also form attachments. When we fall in love, marry, and settle down in a particular neighborhood, we form attachments. Attachments are a necessary aspect of life. God has created us to form them. But we will one day be separated from every attachment, with the one exception of our attachment to God in Christ.

Resolving depression, therefore, is a matter of "disconnecting" from the object to which we have become attached. Some of us are perhaps too attached to life and its material things. Because Jesus understood how we form those attachments, He warned us, "What good will it be for a man if he gains the whole world, yet forfeits his soul?" (Matt. 16:26). The apostle Paul warned us to "set your affection on things above, not on things on the earth" (Col. 3:2, KJV). Those are timely warnings made by a God who knows us well. They need to be heeded if we're going to deal with depression effectively. In other words, it's possible to be too attached to the things of this world for our own good.

The healing of depression ultimately comes when we allow the thing or person to which we're clinging to go free. That's also true for our reputation, our disappointments, and our need to be in control. We will talk more about this in chapter 5.

DO CHRISTIANS HAVE AN ADVANTAGE?

The superiority of our resources as Christians shows clearly in this area. Every disappointment, every criticism, and every person who lets us down or betrays us is an opportunity for God's grace to be at work in us, to produce spiritual growth. We know God is in control! We believe He has a plan for our lives! We've experienced His working in the past. This perspective can help us to release the things of the world and speed up the grieving process.

Let me hasten to add that this is not cause for anyone who is depressed to feel guilty. We're all at different stages in our spiritual growth. Some, like the apostle Paul, can say, "I consider everything a loss compared to the surpassing greatness of knowing Christ Jesus my Lord, for whose sake I have lost all things" (Phil. 3:8). Others will find even minor losses difficult to deal with. God doesn't judge us for that. But He does call us to grow in maturity so we can come to terms with our losses more quickly.

What's important spiritually is not whether we're free of depression, but whether we use each experience of loss as an opportunity to see God's will for our lives more clearly. The majority of us might well have to struggle with every loss we experience. We're slow learners! At times we may be able to demonstrate monumental faith, and even significant traumas won't phase us. At other times, even petty issues will provoke a significant depression. The key to a happy, healthy, and spiritually mature life lies in being able to receive our losses gracefully, grieve them with God's help, and finally get to the place where we become "nonattached" to much of this world.

The ability to deal with loss constructively is a basic mental health skill that everyone ought to develop. We should teach it in kindergarten, reinforce it in adolescence, and continue to develop it throughout life. Our level of happiness and fulfillment depends on it.

DOESN'T THE DEPRESSION EXPERIENCE CARRY WITHIN IT THE SEEDS OF ITS OWN DEEPENING?

It seems logical to think that depression itself is such a significant loss that it creates still more depression, but that's not the case. Depression is not automatically self-perpetuating but tends to move back toward normality. The mind and the body have a self-healing set. Only when this normal depression cycle is interfered with does it get perpetuated. How people think about their loss is the determining factor, the key to healing.

HOW DO ENDOGENOUS DEPRESSIONS DIFFER FROM REACTIVE DEPRESSIONS?

As I explained in the first chapter, endogenous depression is caused by a disturbed biochemistry and can be triggered by many factors, including genetic defect, stress, fatigue, illness, or some glandular malfunctions.

Adrenaline letdown is another common cause, varying from a mild weekend depression to much-more-serious letdowns. Sometimes the period immediately following a success or victory may trigger this kind of depression. We call it a "postadrenaline" depression, because it occurs when our adrenaline suddenly drops after it has been on a high.

Elijah's experience after his stunning victory at Mount Carmel (see 1 Kings 18-19) is a good example of this postexcitement letdown. When he had defeated the prophets of Baal, he ran into the wilderness, lay down under a juniper tree, and asked God to take his life.

This postclimax depression has an important physiological root. During periods of success, we draw heavily on our adrenaline and arousal systems. The moment excess adrenaline is no longer needed, it's as if our systems say, "Now switch off. We need time to recover." In providing that recovery time, then, postadrenaline depressions are very healthy.

Endogenous depressions can also be the most serious form of major depression, the bipolar disorder, formerly known as manic-depressive psychosis. If treated promptly, these depressions can be brought under control rapidly, and unnecessary suffering can be avoided.

WHAT ARE THE MOST COMMON PHYSIOLOGICAL CAUSES OF DEPRESSION?

Glandular problems, fatigue caused by stress, and many illnesses, including cancer and influenza, can cause depression in both men and women. Many medications cause depression as well. In women, the menstrual cycle is a very important cause (see chapter 3). Some physiological causes are mysterious—we haven't yet discovered what they are, although we can see their effects.

CAN DEPRESSIONS BE TRIGGERED BY DRUGS?

Drugs, or more correctly the side effects of drugs, can create depression. Alcohol, for example, may initially alleviate depression and is used by many people as a tranquilizer. When they feel down, they turn to alcohol. But alcohol is actually a depressant, so after it wears off, the depression is worse than before. Other drugs stimulate the system. They create a feeling of well-being, but not for long. The depression is worse when the drug wears off.

IS DEPRESSION HEREDITARY?

Some forms of depression are clearly hereditary. That's especially true for the major endogenous depressions. Studies of identical twins, for example, have clearly established a genetic link. Whether all depressions that run in families are due to heredity, we don't know, because we haven't been able to identify the specific mechanism of onset.

Some minor endogenous depressions aren't necessarily genetic but are caused instead by overstress or malfunction in the endocrine system. Some evidence suggests, however, that in people who experience a psychological depression over a long period, the body becomes adapted to that low level of functioning. The biochemical disturbance becomes relatively permanent, but it is brought about by a lifetime of depressive living.

Sometimes parents teach their children to deal with life in a depressive style. Those parents were taught the same patterns by their own parents, so the problem gets passed from generation to generation.

Generally speaking, genetic depressions respond well to antidepressant treatment. My opinion is that it's better to suffer from one of the genetically caused depressions (that can be treated) than from the neurotic forms that are more difficult to overcome.

WHAT IS THE RELATIONSHIP BETWEEN LOW BLOOD SUGAR AND DEPRESSION?

Many people report feelings of depression or low mood some time after they have eaten or, more commonly, just before their next meal. That is caused by a low blood-sugar level, and some are more sensitive to it than others. Low blood sugar disrupts our whole emotional balance. We become irritable, intolerant, or easily angered. Blood-sugar problems can often precipitate depression, too, because our social environment is disturbed.

Consider this familiar scenario. Your husband comes home from work. You haven't been able to grab a bite since early morning because you've been too busy. The low blood sugar makes you irritable. There's a bit of a quarrel, and your husband storms out. You feel a sense of loss, and you become depressed. Your depression is not caused by the low blood sugar, but by the secondary consequences of it. This is the kind of complex cycle that can disturb our emotional balance.

CAN DIET CONTRIBUTE TO A TENDENCY TOWARD DEPRESSION?

Some people contend that diet is an important component in depression. Certainly, if our diets are not well balanced, or if we're deficient in certain essential vitamins, our systems are not going to cope satisfactorily with life. The consequence is ultimately depression. Some hold that sugar intensifies the cyclical highs and lows of our emotions with its "artificial highs," but that's an overstatement for those who are not diabetic. On balance, though, good nutrition is important for physiological well-being, so it's probably also good for mental well-being.

WHAT IS THE RELATIONSHIP BETWEEN PHYSICAL FITNESS AND DEPRESSION?

Evidence suggests that physical exercise is very important in maintaining a balanced emotional life. Well-exercised, energetic bodies function much more efficiently than physically inactive bodies, and fit people cope better with stress and are not as prone to illness. Some psychiatric hospitals, in fact, use exercise programs for severely depressed patients, because exercise acts as a stimulant to the system. Thus, exercise is helpful in both avoiding and treating depression. It doesn't replace standard treatment but augments it.

DO CERTAIN ILLNESSES CAUSE DEPRESSION DIRECTLY?

Very much so. For example, depression is a common symptom of influenza. The depression helps the healing process by slowing us down and causing us to be disinterested in our usual activities. Certain forms of cancer create deep depressions, although in the case of life-threatening illnesses, many threatened and real losses must be contended with as well. In those cases, depression is a protective mechanism. It removes us from life, slows us down, and makes us disinterested in our environment so our bodies can have the time needed to fight the illness.

HOW CAN WE DEAL WITH THE DEPRESSION THAT ACCOMPANIES AGING?

Depression does not have to be a part of aging, but many elderly people do get depressed. Not only does your body change, limiting your ability to do the things you used to do, but you also begin to feel a shortness of time; a sense of things coming to an end increases your awareness of the limits of life. It hurts to lose your job when you're young, but it's not nearly as catastrophic as losing your job near the end of your working life. So all sorts of adjustments are needed to the losses associated with aging.

Adjusting to the aging process as healthily and realistically as possible involves an acceptance of the facts of aging—that we all have to get old and eventually die. You can't go backward in life; you can only go forward. And again, as a Christian psychologist, I believe we have wonderful resources available to us in this process. Getting old is not as bleak a prospect for us as it is for those who don't believe in God.

The best possible adjustment for advancing age is to be well in the previous stage. If your adolescent years were well adjusted, for example, your early adult years are likely to be well adjusted. If they were not, you'll experience problems in the next stage. Each stage builds on the previous one. It may seem this fact holds out little hope for the older person who has not adjusted well previously. *The reality, however, is that it's never too late to begin.* Make the most of your present stage in life. That's the best way to assure you adjust well to the final stage.

IS MUCH OF WHAT IS PASSED OFF AS SENILITY IN OLD AGE REALLY DEPRESSION?

Senility and depression are different phenomena, but it's difficult to separate the two. There's no doubt that senile disorders tend to create a lot of depression. How much is physiological and how much is psychological isn't always clear. When someone develops a senile disorder like Alzheimer's disease, many losses can accompany a decline in mental abilities. These include the loss of friends and the loss of activities. Such losses can cause depression as well as the physical changes that occur in the brain. The two are so interwoven that it's difficult to separate one from the other.

HOW DO NEUROTIC DEPRESSIONS DIFFER FROM OTHERS?

Neurotic depressions are caused by inadequate responses to life's demands. They normally build up over a long period into a life-style pattern, and they're neurotic because they're an unhealthy way of coping with anxieties and pressures. This type of depression has now become known as dysthymic disorder, although I don't like that label.

WHAT ARE THE CHARACTERISTICS
OF A DEPRESSIVE LIFE-STYLE?

Many people retreat into depression to avoid dealing with the pressures of life. After years of this retreating, they develop a life-style of cowardice. Every time they encounter a bit of tension, stress, or anxiety, they withdraw into depression. They wake up in the morning, and the prospect of facing the day is overwhelming. So they retreat and stay in bed all day.

The characteristics of this life-style include a tendency toward depression at the slightest hint of anxiety, a low tolerance for stress, avoidance behavior, and a nonengagement of life. I must sound one important qualification, however. Sometimes perpetual depression is a symptom of a more serious endogenous depression. Before we can interpret persistent depressions as a neurotic life-style, we must eliminate the possibility that the depression is due to physiological disturbance.

T H R E E

Women and Depression

S tudies of both psychiatric patients and the general population indicate that depression is more common among women than men. According to a report in the *Stanford Observer*, women suffer from serious depression at about twice the rate of men. Further, one of every four American women will be affected by depression at some time in her life. Of all the women who get depressed, probably no two have exactly the same circumstances, and they experience a wide variety of feelings, thoughts, and behaviors.

Many don't even know they're depressed and suffer through life with rather severe penalties from a personal and social point of view. They are probably shunned and don't have many friends because of their frequent depressions. If depression is now at epidemic proportions in our culture in general, it's especially true for women.

Clearly, we need a better understanding of the unique depressions that affect women.

WHY DO WOMEN GET DEPRESSED MORE OFTEN THAN MEN?

There's a lot of argument about why that is. Many theories have been proposed, ranging from social conditions and income differences to biological reasons and hormones. No single theory is more correct than another. They're probably all correct to some extent and together explain it better than by themselves.

Before I go any further, let me first address the validity of the statistic that women get depressed twice as often as men. Some have challenged it on the grounds that there is a bias in the reporting and gathering of data from women. Many believe depression labels are used more frequently with women than with men. There's no doubt in my mind that in times past, and probably to some extent today, there has been a negative bias toward women when it comes to psychological or psychiatric diagnosis. Women are more likely to be diagnosed as severely disturbed than men, often by predominantly male mental health workers.

In recent years, however, that bias has been corrected by the consciousness raising of those who have tried to make the system more fair toward women. Further, the mental health profession is now well populated with women. Yet the statistic that women are more depression prone still exists.

What are the basic causes of depression in women?

I'll provide a brief overview of the major causes and then pick up on the more serious ones in detail through the rest of the chapter.

1. Social Factors

For a long time, social conditions and attitudes in our culture have worked to the disadvantage of women. Girls were taught to be dependent and submissive, and a unique state of helplessness was fostered. Depression, for many women, has had to become a survival strategy. In other words, when living conditions are intolerable, many women retreat into depression, show an indifference to their environment, and become passive and helpless as the only way they can cope.

This is particularly true when physical abuse is present. Current estimates are that somewhere between 2 and 6 million women in the United States are battered annually. A high percentage of those women are victims of incest. Further, large numbers of women are raped and/or killed by their husbands or boyfriends. Such social conditions clearly have a serious impact on the state of mind of the average woman, and depression is often the only way these women can deal with their situations.

2. Role Changes Affecting Women

Many role changes are taking place for women. They are increasingly assuming leadership positions in government, industry, business, and even the church. More and more are becoming the primary breadwinners in their families. It's not uncommon to encounter women who are earning significantly more than their husbands. The family's financial well-being is thus more and more dependent on the wife's income. With the increasing incidence of divorce, ever more women find themselves as the sole support of a family of children, so they must be more than just mothers. The daily work load and stress of playing these many roles can take their toll in the form of biological and emotional breakdowns.

3. Problems with Self-Esteem

The connection between diminished self-esteem and depression has long been known. Depression not only causes low self-esteem, but anyone whose esteem has been eroded is likely to be more prone to depression as well. In our culture, women clearly tend to experience lower self-esteem than men.

Partly this is because while there are greater opportunities for success, women are less likely to be successful. Partly it's due to the lower social status of women, who tend to earn less money for equivalent types of work. But largely it's due to being female in a male-dominated culture. Maleness is preferred over femaleness in many sectors of our society, and this bias is even greater against women of color.

Of course, changes are taking place. In many sectors of society, opportunities for women have increased dramatically. But it's still going to be several generations before we see a change in stereotypes and basic attitudes toward women that won't work to erode their self-esteem and put them at greater risk for depression.

4. Biological Factors

The reproductive function of women has contributed heavily to their greater incidence of depression. Not that all the consequences related to the reproductive function are biological. Problems with infertility, singleness (and thus not being able to bear children), and trying to find the right partner in life are all tied to some extent to the reproductive burden of the female and are likely to cause serious psychological deficits.

By far the more serious and common consequence of the reproduction function lies in the complex hormonal and physiological changes that support it. The two most serious biological consequences are *PMS* and *menopause*. They will be given careful attention later in this chapter.

Some people emphatically reject the biological explanation for depression in women. They don't deny that some women have serious problems with hormones, but they insist that hormones don't influence moods in most women. They would also argue that men and women are equally susceptible to depression but that depression in males often takes the form of acting out behaviors such as passivity, crying, or even alcoholism, and that this accounts for the apparent difference.

We certainly need more research before we can make categorical statements about how biological factors contribute to depression proneness. For now, there seems to be sufficient evidence to suggest that at least for a percentage of American women, biological factors do play a major role in their emotions.

WHAT ARE SOME OF THE RISK FACTORS FOR WOMEN?

Whether a particular form of depression is entirely psychological and caused by social factors or biological and caused by hormonal changes, significant factors can make the risk for depression greater. In other words, psychological and biological factors often work in tandem to produce a given state of depression. What are these risk factors?

1. Living Alone

According to the 1980 U.S. census, almost 11 million women over 14 years of age live alone (i.e., with no other adult). Of those, more than 8 million are single mothers who live with their 11 million children. Clearly, these are courageous, skillful, flexible, and resourceful women. They live highly stressed and demanding lives. They have to be breadwinner, parent, homemaker, and friend, and then try to find a little time to take care of themselves. Most of these women, whether rich or poor, regardless of race or profession, are in some kind of pain. Living alone, according to statistics, doubles the risk of depression.

To avoid being at increased risk for depression, single women and especially single mothers need to develop an adequate base of friendships and social contacts. Isolation fosters too much introspection and does not provide enough balancing distraction to control moods. Women tend to pay more attention to their feelings and are more likely to ruminate about the possible causes of their moods. Isolation only makes matters worse.

Overall, men seem to have better social support systems than women. When depressed, men tend to engage in activities designed to distract themselves from their moods, whereas women tend to engage in activities that might intensify their moods.

Even married women can be socially isolated. I have received numerous letters from women who say that even though they're married, they're extremely lonely. Their husbands hardly ever talk to them and seldom take them out to social events. Such women, like single women, can be at increased risk for depression unless they build an adequate network of friends and participate in regular social activities outside the home.

2. Sexual Desirability

Since our culture primarily puts the responsibility on women to be attractive to men in order to date and marry, many women are at increased risk for depression if they don't see themselves as sexually desirable. That leads to an increased preoccupation with their bodies, appearance, and how they're perceived by men. Eating disorders are mainly a women's problem and relate clearly to concerns about weight and negative feelings toward the body. Indirectly, this also affects self-worth and perceptions of one's desirability.

3. Lack of Identity

For many women, especially those who don't develop careers of their own, their identities become too wrapped up in playing mother and housewife. If anything happens to disturb those roles or to take them away, depression can be a serious problem.

Our egos become defined by what we do. A good mother who takes care of her children, teaches them good manners, and finally delivers them into adulthood as successful people will find her identity seriously diminished when they're gone. We call this the "empty nest syndrome," but it's more than just an empty nest that puts this type of mother at risk for depression. It's the sense of emptiness and lack of fulfillment that sets in when she's no longer needed. Suddenly she finds herself all alone, adrift in a huge ocean with no direction and no sense of accomplishment. That increases the risk of depression. It's also about this time that menopause sets in to further complicate the picture.

Women who divorce later in life also experience this reaction of isolation and abandonment. When you've spent 20 or 25 years of your life building a home for your husband and children so they can retreat from their busy and stressed lives to a harbor of peace and contentment, the rejection is devastating. When you have provided meals, nursed a sick husband and children through critical illnesses, and then suddenly find yourself cast aside, the depression you experience is more than just the loss of a marriage. It's the loss of identity. Your very essence is destroyed.

The sad thing about this is that it can be prevented. While I highly value the role of motherhood and of building and maintaining a happy home, women need to develop a stronger sense of their own identity outside the home. They need other levels of competence besides that of homemaking.

My wife, Kathleen, is a good example of this. She has provided myself and our three daughters with a wonderful home. She has served us diligently, and she has, besides all that, worked hard to develop her own self and achieve a feeling of competency that complements being a good mother and housewife.

After raising three children, Kathleen began to look around for other opportunities for fulfillment. She also felt a need to do something of her own choosing. So she enrolled in Fuller Seminary to take a few courses. She didn't want the pressure of pursuing a degree, but she did want to enhance her spiritual growth.

When she completed those courses, she began working part-time for a missionary organization, developing a project for starving children in Africa. That project gave her a great sense of fulfillment, and it also helped her realize where her gifts lay: she felt called to work with other women. At the same time, God opened an opportunity for her to start a weekly Bible study and prayer meeting with seminary students' wives, and she's been doing that with joy for the past six years. In addition, she now speaks with me at seminars, and she also has four grandchildren to love.

Every husband owes it to his wife to foster such development, and certainly every woman owes it to herself to claim it. Without an identity broader than simply taking care of home and husband, any woman is at greater risk for depression. That's not to say women must live in fear of being abandoned. I certainly pray you will never experience the rejection of your spouse. But there are some events in life over which a woman has no control. Her children will leave her one day, and her spouse may succumb to disease. But even if her children never leave and her husband outlives her, she needs a clear sense of her own identity and a feeling of competence so she can define who she is out of a much broader base.

HOW CAN I DO THIS?

• As soon as you're able, go back to school and enjoy the personal growth and mind enhancement education can provide.

• Become an avid reader. Books are a wonderful resource for expanding your mind and developing your identity.

• Engage in volunteer work, and give yourself in service to people outside your home.

• Maintain a strong commitment to spiritual development, which addresses issues of identity and provides a much broader perspective on our lives and on the function and roles we play in the lives of family members.

• Keep communication open with your husband about your needs for identity and to feel you are a growing person. Ask your husband to participate in fostering your growth. That will avoid feelings he might have that you're neglecting your family responsibilities.

HOW DOES THE PREMENSTRUAL
SYNDROME AFFECT WOMEN?

For the last ten of her 28 years, Paula has lived a split life. Half of every month, she's an attractive, intelligent, well-adjusted, and happy woman. But for the two weeks preceding her menstrual period, she's a physical and emotional wreck. In particular, she experiences extreme mood swings that cause dramatic personality changes.

During the "good" part of her month, she is composed, competent at her job as a social worker, and easy to get along with. She and her husband hardly ever fight. During the second half of her month, she becomes wildly irrational, deeply depressed, and aggressive. She picks a fight over anything, has put her fist through several doors, has tried to slash her wrists, and has had one serious car accident.

Paula suffers from a common form of depression, the one that accompanies the premenstrual syndrome (PMS). Of course, PMS has many other accompanying physical and emotional problems as well. But for Paula, the experience of depression is the dominant symptom and the one that causes her the greatest amount of distress. It's one of the forms of depression that is unique to being a woman.

Many women have learned to accept and live with PMS. Others have had to resort to hysterectomies, while still others need intensive treatment for its many symptoms.

Premenstrual syndrome is probably the most common cause of biological depressions in women. In recent years, many studies have turned up helpful facts about it, and whereas years ago doctors suggested that the problem was mainly psychosomatic and aggravated by neurotic tendencies, no one believes that anymore. It is a *real* problem, and its cause is primarily, if not exclusively, biological.

As recently as 1981, the *American Journal of Obstetrics and Gynecology* reported that between 20 and 40 percent of American women were afflicted with some mental or physical incapacity during their menstrual periods. How many of those women had PMS? Dr. Katharina Dalton, a London physician who has been treating PMS for 30 years, believes as many as 5.5 million American women (about 10% of the population of childbearing age) have the disorder to a degree that calls for medical help.[1] For some, it is so severe that their violent mood swings can disrupt their lives and the lives of their families.

Since the early 1980s, of course, we have made even greater strides toward understanding and treating PMS. Gone are the days, we hope, when doctors, psychiatrists, and psychologists tell women with PMS that there's nothing wrong with

---

1. *Family Circle*, June 4, 1982, p. 28.

them and that all they need to do is pull themselves together. There *is* something wrong. They are not neurotic. They have a real physiological disorder that needs consistent and aggressive treatment just like any other.

The emotional effects of PMS that accompany the physical (e.g., headaches, clumsiness, pain, and even seizures) are primarily depression, fatigue, tension, anxiety, and irritability. I want to focus primarily on depression, since that's the main focus of this book and is often overshadowed by the more dramatic symptoms of anger and irritability.

Because no woman has all the symptoms associated with PMS, periods of depression can often be overlooked as a significant feature of the disorder, which is rapidly becoming stereotyped as a problem of tension and anger. As one patient described it, "It's like being possessed, I guess. Whenever I'm close to my period I fly off at my husband, I lash out at my children, I rip clothing, smash glasses, throw crockery, and even take a hammer to my prized vases. I feel totally out of control, and when it's all over I feel so ashamed."

WHAT ARE THE OTHER SYMPTOMS?

Many women experience sadness and depression—significant enough to impair their lives. They feel listless and without energy. They lose all interest in normal activities, and they begin to think about themselves in self-demeaning terms. They cry excessively and then start to entertain thoughts of taking their own lives. Death wishes are extremely common during these periods.

Such an unpleasant mood can precipitate other problems, such as drug abuse and alcoholism. Many turn to alcohol, for instance, as a way of numbing their feelings and taking away their emotional pain. The depression as well as the other symptoms of PMS can lead to marital discord and child abuse and can make the sufferer prone to accidents.

WHAT CAUSES PMS?

It is generally agreed that the primary cause of PMS is an insufficiency of the female hormone progesterone, normally produced by the ovaries to prepare the lining of the uterus for pregnancy. The primary medical treatment, therefore, is to replace the deficient progesterone, a strategy that has taken a long time to become accepted in the United States. Many clinics are now available to provide this treatment, and many physicians offer it as well.

If you suffer from severe depression as a result of PMS, therefore, your first response should be to seek treatment for this underlying deficiency. Attention also has to be given to blood-sugar fluctuations and vitamin deficiencies, and treatment invariably includes some education about stress management and preventive strategies.

HOW DOES PMS DIFFER FROM
PMT (PREMENSTRUAL TENSION)?

Not every woman suffers acutely enough from PMS to need progesterone supplement treatment. It's important to distinguish between the severe form of the disorder, which has clear clinical manifestations both physically and emotionally, and "premenstrual tension" or distress. This latter term describes the discomfort some women feel during their menstrual cycle that tends to get worse around the time of menstruation but in which the hormonal balance is quite normal and so progesterone does not help at all.

In other words, premenstrual tension is a minor form of PMS and is probably a lot more common than we realize. For instance, I've seen women in therapy who have never thought of themselves as having a PMS problem yet who say they become significantly depressed at some time in the month. Because it never coincides exactly with menstruation, they have never seen it as being connected in any way. Generally they are able to control their emotions, and it seldom gets beyond being a personal discomfort. Family members don't notice it particularly, but the sufferer experiences a fair degree of misery.

HOW CAN I TELL IF MY DEPRESSION
IS RELATED TO PMT?

How can a woman know whether she experiences this milder form of PMS? The only effective way I know is to keep a daily "mood diary" and carefully chart how you're feeling. For instance, you could think of a scale from 0 to 10 for your general feeling of well being. A 0 would mean you're feeling absolutely terrible, down in the dumps, extremely depressed, whereas 10 is the highest feeling of well being you've ever experienced when you're free of all sadness and life seems to be happiest. A 5 would be somewhere in between, where you feel neither extremely happy nor very depressed.

At the end of each day, give yourself a rating between 0 and 10 for how you felt most of the day. If anything particularly devastating or disappointing has happened, make a note of it as well, because that may account for why your mood is down. If nothing significant has happened, your rating is more likely to reflect accurately your general mood as determined by your body's chemistry.

Whenever you have a period, mark the starting and ending dates in your diary. After several months of keeping such a diary, it should become clear at what time of the month your depression sets in, as well as how long it lasts. Knowing there's a connection between your depression and your body chemistry can free you from a lot of false blame and avoid the unnecessary searching of your environment for explanations. This keeps the depression at its lowest common denominator, namely, as a biological one. It does not exaggerate it or produce other, secondary psychological reactions that can make it worse.

CAN YOU SUGGEST SOME SELF-HELPS?

What can you do for yourself when you realize you're in a period of depression tied to premenstrual variations? Here are some suggestions:

1. Life-Style Changes

The unpleasant physical symptoms of your PMS can be relieved by minor changes in life-style. For example, bloating, painful breasts, weight gain, and headaches often result from water retention. They cause enough discomfort to add extra pain to the emotional depression you already feel. By minimizing the bloating with, for example, a diet low in carbohydrates and salt, you can reduce the amount of water held in the body. That reduces the physical discomfort and may help to improve your mood. You might want to discuss with your doctor whether a mild diuretic (this removes water from the body), taken a week or so before your expected premenstrual emotional change, can be helpful.

2. Dietary Changes

Changes in diet can help significantly in lowering your mood swings. Stimulants such as those contained in caffeine-based foods, coffee, tea, colas, and chocolate will help to reduce tension and anxiety. Some have also found it helpful to eat more but smaller meals each day during the premenstrual period, keeping the calorie intake the same but not loading the gastrointestinal system with large meals. This helps to balance blood-sugar levels that bring on headaches when they drop suddenly.

Although there is no scientific proof of its usefulness, some have found vitamin B6 to be helpful as well.

3. Exercise

Regular exercise clearly benefits women with PMS in any of its forms, because it helps to tone up the body and aids in relaxation. It also helps to burn off surplus adrenaline, thus lowering stress levels.

4. Stress Control

Stress significantly aggravates the problem of PMS. Not only do the hormonal deficiencies associated with PMS reduce your tolerance for stress, but prolonged and chronic stress also affects the endocrine system and will aggravate any existing deficiency. The body cannot fight all its battles at the same time. During times of high stress, adrenaline levels increase, muscle tension goes up, and blood volume is shifted within the body to those regions that require it for the emergency response (the brain, the stomach, the muscles, and the lungs).

Those changes, taken together, will reduce the body's ability to cope with the primary hormonal deficiency that underlies PMS. Stress will, therefore, make matters worse. Good stress management is thus essential, as is learning an effective relaxation exercise that will help to lower the body's adrenaline level and reduce its emergency mode.

CAN YOU SUGGEST A GOOD RELAXATION EXERCISE?

Relaxation can be achieved by spending a minimum of 30 minutes a day in a quiet place, totally relaxing your body and mind. Start at the bottom of your body with your feet; tense the foot muscles for five seconds, and then relax them. Move to your calves, and do the same. Proceed up the body and through the various muscle systems, first tensing them for five seconds and then relaxing them, until you have covered the whole body.

Having done that, remain immobile for the balance of the relaxation time. Try not to move any muscle. It helps to set a timer for 20 or 30 minutes and to put a "Do not disturb" sign on your door. You certainly can't relax while you have small children running around or teenagers barging in and asking for favors. Even your spouse needs to stay away. At the end of your relaxation time, take a few deep breaths, and then go about your business.

Other activities, such as slow swimming or lying in a Jacuzzi, can also help to create a more relaxed body.

Stress management is mostly a matter of "filtering" your stressors and trying to concentrate only on essential issues. Many helpful resources are available, and I would refer the reader to my book *Adrenalin and Stress*,[2] which provides some strategies for doing this.

---

2. Archibald D. Hart, *Adrenalin and Stress* (Dallas: Word, 1986).

HOW DOES MENOPAUSE RELATE TO DEPRESSION?

Perhaps you have just encountered the depression of menopause, suffering from it yourself or knowing someone who does. Maybe your first thought is *How could this happen to me?* Let me immediately assure you that of all the depressions afflicting women, this is one of the most common. It comes in all sizes, from just minor sadnesses to major melancholy. It's associated with the change of life, and, not surprisingly, it affects *both* men and women. However, since it is more serious in women, I'll focus my discussion on them.

There's nothing unnatural about menopause. It's not a disease, and it's not a sign of weakness. Instead, it is the perfectly natural cessation of the reproduction process provided by creation. It serves an important function, namely, to prevent the birth of an unhealthy or deficient child to a woman whose body and hormones are probably not adequate to produce a healthy child. It also ensures that the child is not born to someone too elderly to take adequate care of him or her. It's all part of an intelligent creation.

For a long time, it was believed that no woman should expect discomfort or emotional upheaval during menopause. The problem was thought to be purely psychological, and it reflected an inadequate earlier adjustment in life. I don't believe that to be true. Most menopausal problems are *entirely* biological and have to do with the natural decline of estrogen and the cessation of child-bearing ability.

Menopause typically begins sometime after age 40, although there is evidence that the age has been dropping, just as the age of puberty has dropped over the past 75 or 100 years. About 50 percent of women experience significant depression during the menopausal period, and for some this process of change can drag on for a long time.

Physicians have a list of dreadful symptoms that may accompany menopause: hot flashes due to instability of the circulatory system; palpitations, or forceful beating of the heart, which may produce shortness of breath; stomach and bowel upsets; headaches; arthritis; fatigue; and even diabetes.

By the time of menopause, many women are worried about being overweight. Instead of switching to a sensible diet, they often take to some fad diet that deprives their bodies of adequate nutrition. That can significantly aggravate menopausal symptoms. Others may drink large quantities of coffee, and I mean the real strong stuff, in the hopes that it will suppress hunger pangs. They skip breakfast and generally ignore the rules for good eating.

Deficiencies produced by these habits can also aggravate menopausal symptoms, as well as produce significant vitamin deficiencies, especially in vitamin E and the B complexes. This almost guarantees increased nervousness, digestive disorders, headaches, and fatigue.

HOW LONG DOES MENOPAUSAL DEPRESSION LAST?

The depression of menopause can be quite variable. It can last just a few days and then go away as mysteriously as it came, or it can last for months and even extend into years. I have seen cases where the biological stress of menopause has triggered a full-blown, major depression requiring intensive therapy and extensive medication. Fortunately, we have effective treatments for the variety of depressions experienced during menopause, so a sufferer needs to be encouraged right at the outset to seek appropriate treatment.

Remember, it's not just your imagination. You're not exaggerating your ailments, God has not abandoned you, and you certainly are not failing as a Christian. Those ideas are ridiculous, and any attempt to blame yourself for your unpleasant and sad feelings will only contribute to further depression by creating more losses. If your depression is incapacitating, you should seek out an understanding doctor to help you immediately.

SHOULD I SEE MY FAMILY DOCTOR, OR DO I NEED A SPECIALIST?

Not all doctors are good at treating menopausal depression. You may need to go to someone other than your regular family doctor. You should first consult a gynecologist, since this physician is especially trained to deal with the problems of menopause. If, after the first visit, you don't feel comfortable with the gynecologist you have selected, move on quickly to try someone else. You may also need to see a psychiatrist. Many gynecologists are extremely good at treating biological aspects of menopause but may not be very understanding or skilled at treating the emotional components.

Be frank with your doctor. Ask whether he or she can adequately treat your depression. In severe cases, it may be necessary for the gynecologist to consult with a psychiatrist to find the right balance of medication. Of course, don't wait until you have a full-blown depression before you seek help. As soon as you begin having hot flashes, heart palpitations, prolonged insomnia, extreme irritability, painful joints, vaginal dryness, excessive or irregular vaginal bleeding, or chronic fatigue even though you've had sufficient rest, consult your physician right away.

In treating menopausal depression, two important aspects must constantly be borne in mind. There's the biological aspect, the diminished estrogen and other female hormones. Then there's the psychological aspect. In other words, the underlying primary biological depression can have a significant overlay of reactive, or psychological, depression.

After all, we don't enjoy growing old, and the menopause can signal the loss of many significant aspects of a woman's life. It means the end of childbearing, so a woman who was hoping to have another child could become depressed because of that. For many women, the loss of childbearing ability also represents a significant loss of meaningfulness. These and many other losses can accompany the realization that menopause is the end of a period of life and contribute additional depression.

It is very possible, therefore, that your treating physician may suggest you seek counseling or psychotherapy as a part of the treatment package. If your physician recommends that, or if you feel a lot of your depression is being caused by losses you aren't coping with satisfactorily, seek out a counselor or psychologist to help you. I strongly recommend that you begin by talking to your pastor for a referral. Here again, the key to prompt recovery is to seek out treatment promptly. That's true for all depressions.

IS THERE ANYTHING ELSE I CAN DO?

Adjusting to a new stage of life can mean the opening up of whole new areas of exciting adventure. You need to look on the bright side of these transitions in life. They may represent the loss of some things, but they're also the beginning of many new experiences. A readjustment of your attitude and elimination of irrational beliefs about being a childbearer can help to speed your recovery.

In addition to the treatment the physician may prescribe, such as estrogen replacement therapy, it may be necessary to add an antidepressant for the more severe cases of depression. You may want to try the estrogen replacement therapy first, but don't wait too long. Antidepressant medications are *not addicting,* nor do they cause any harm if you take them and don't really need them. Generally I advise women to at least try an antidepressant early in the treatment process. If you don't get the biological depression under control, it will likely exacerbate any psychological depression caused by the menopause.

If your physician has recommended against estrogen replacement therapy because of the risk of tumors, high blood pressure, diabetes, or other disorders, you may be entirely dependent upon the antidepressant to help you through your depression.

There's one comforting thought you can hold on to: all menopausal depressions ultimately come to an end. You can look forward to a point in the future when your discomfort will be behind you. Menopause is only a milestone in your life, not the whole journey. It can be a time to rededicate yourself to a more-purposeful and productive life in Christ. It is certainly not the time for self-pity or self-punishment. Turn your temporary affliction into an opportunity for growth.

WHAT IS POSTPARTUM DEPRESSION?

A special form of depression women are prone to is the one that follows childbirth. Commonly it is known as the "baby blues," but technically it's *postpartum depression*. Like menopause, this depression was viewed for a long time as a neurotic disorder, and women were blamed for not being adequately prepared for motherhood. They were, supposedly, afraid of the responsibility. In a few cases that might be true, but for the majority of cases, the problem is again biological. Most mothers embrace their children and become bonded in such a way that makes for a happy child-rearing reaction.

The intensity of the postpartum depression can vary from mild, where one may just feel a little down for a few days, to severe psychosis, where one is incapable of taking care of the child. The more severe the depression, the more clearly it is caused by biological factors. But even milder forms can be caused by fatigue and the hormonal changes that accompany childbirth. Postpartum depression is not confined to first-time mothers, either. Some women have a period of depression following the birth of each child. Others only have it sometimes.

Almost every mother goes through a few "low" days after the birth of a child. This coincides roughly with the time it takes for the breasts to begin to produce milk. Many more women, however, experience a more severe depression when they leave the hospital. Sometimes this is due to just being physically run down, but often it's caused by the hormonal changes that follow childbirth.

DOES POSTPARTUM DEPRESSION REQUIRE TREATMENT?

Only the severest depressions require treatment. Among the most common feelings experienced in postpartum depression are insecurity, fear of inability to cope with the baby, disappointment about the child's sex or appearance, confusion, general fears, and anxiety. Young mothers with postpartum depression need to resist believing there is something wrong with them. Certainly, there may be something wrong with their hormones, but that doesn't reflect on them as people.

Questioning your ability to be a loving and caring mother or feeling guilty about not being the perfect mother will certainly aggravate your depression. To help you limit those thoughts and control your feelings, a brief period of counseling may be extremely helpful. Ask your pastor or physician for a referral to a competent therapist, preferably a woman who can help you sort out your feelings and prevent you from creating further losses. If you can receive emotional support and reassurance from your family, friends, mother, or counselor, the chances are that the depression will quickly pass and your recovery will be complete.

Whatever you do, don't overglorify motherhood. Being a mother is hard work, and not every baby is the perfect child. Just accept the reality of what it takes to be a mother and you'll cope a lot better. In a short while, your feelings will return to normal.

F O U R

Depression in Children and Adolescents

O ne important study has shown that at any one time, as many as 20 children in 100 (one in five) may be suffering from significant symptoms of depression.[1] This may seem an alarmingly high figure, but when you realize many of these children manifest their depression in some sort of "masked" form, it's not that difficult to accept.

For many children, their depressions are temporary and don't require any special treatment. They are caused by normal losses every child has to come to terms with. Children lose pets who run into the road and get killed; friends move away; relatives die; sometimes they can't get what they want. Those are all losses children have to get through, but because they haven't yet developed the skills for coping with significant losses, they invariably go into some form of depression.

Childhood depressions can also be very serious, not only because of the intensity of the depressions, but also because children are almost totally incapable of responding to their environment and making the appropriate adjustments to loss.

Perhaps the most important point to make about childhood depression is that it's in those early stages of development that the patterns for later depressions are laid. The way a child comes to terms with frustration and learns how to handle loss sets the stage for how depressions are handled later in life, particularly in the

---

1. Archibald D. Hart, *Counseling the Depressed* (Waco, Tex.: Word, 1987), p. 150.

neurotic and reactive depressions.

If you sense your child is depressed, please don't hesitate to get help. Between your support and that of a caring professional, your child can emerge a stronger, healthier person.

WHAT IS CHILDHOOD DEPRESSION?

Reaching consensus on an adequate definition of childhood depression is a real problem. Some researchers will only classify as a depression a mood disorder that is totally incapacitating. On the other hand, I believe depression embraces the full range from a normal experience of sadness all the way through to a major depression. It's not always easy to draw a line between what's normal and what is clinically a problem. For a child, however, it probably doesn't make any difference. Depression is depression. And when a child is sad, what's important is that he or she learns how to deal with that sadness in a healthy manner.

WHAT ARE THE SYMPTOMS OF CHILDHOOD DEPRESSION?

While adults show their depression clearly as an intense sadness, a tendency to cry a lot, loss of energy, and social withdrawal, children don't always show theirs so straightforwardly. Here are some of the ways a child manifests depression:

- sadness
- withdrawal—the child will not converse or play with friends
- no interest in regular activities or games
- a profound loss of energy
- complaints about being tired all the time
- little capacity for pleasure
- many physical complaints, ranging from stomachache to headache to vague pains all over the body
- complaints about feeling unloved or rejected
- refusal to receive comfort or love, even though protesting not being loved
- many thoughts about death and dying
- an increase in aggressive behavior, bickering, and negativity
- many sleep disturbances, including insomnia
- a change in appetite, either overeating or refusing to eat favorite foods

An appetite disorder called *anorexia nervosa*, which involves a rejection of food and an avoidance of eating, is frequently a symptom of depression in older girls.

One factor in childhood depression that's different from adult depression is the increased sensitivity children have in relating to their peers. They are very concerned about how they're seen by friends, and any rejection they perceive causes or aggravates depression.

The features of adult depression that are normally absent in childhood include dread of the future and inability to respond quickly to external change or distractions. Unlike adults, children *do* respond when you take them somewhere for a treat or change their environment. They have not yet learned the neurotic tendencies of adults, who see any change in environment simply as a temporary distraction.

We need to be alert to the *hidden symptoms* of childhood depression. These include extreme forms of anxiety, nail biting, hair pulling or twirling, muscle tics, irritability, temper tantrums, sulkiness or moodiness, excessive negativity, self-mutilation, and deliberate destructive behavior. They can all mask a significant childhood depression.

WHAT ARE THE CAUSES OF CHILDHOOD DEPRESSION?

There are many causes for childhood depression, but as with adult depression, they all reduce to one essential theme: the experience of loss. Let's look at one example.

Reggie is only 11, but he behaves as if he's much older. He has seen quite a bit of life. Ever since he can remember, his parents have argued and fought. They separated many times. Sometimes his mother left home and took him with her to a hotel room for several weeks. At other times his father left home, leaving Reggie alone with his mother. On one occasion, he took Reggie with him.

Because of this topsy-turvy home life, Reggie learned early to fend for himself. He tried not to show too much pain, and whenever the conflict between his parents became too intense, he would retreat to his bedroom or take a long walk until the conflict had subsided. As a result, Reggie became a very lonely person. He didn't like to be around his friends, at least the few he had, because they asked him all sorts of embarrassing questions about his family life.

Slowly the tension began to get to Reggie. He discovered that if he just retreated into himself, he could anesthetize his feelings. By the time he became 11, he was adept at switching off and not paying much attention to the bickering between his parents that sometimes erupted into physical violence. He lost interest in games, seldom went out other than to go to school, and even neglected the television set. The only activity he allowed himself was to listen to the stereo in his room with headphones on. This helped to shut out the world and to numb his feelings.

What's wrong with Reggie? Clearly, he is depressed. In fact, by the time his mother realized something was wrong and sought help, Reggie had already developed an intense clinical depression. He had become so "slowed down" that his mother thought there was something physically wrong with him. "He has absolutely no energy," she complained to me. "He just lies around all the time and says he's too tired to do anything."

Reggie had also lost interest in other activities, including his hobbies and the games he liked to play. He had begun to make threats about taking his life or wishing he were dead. A dark, gloomy mood had come over him, and his mother was frightened.

It's not hard to understand what depression is all about when you observe its development in a young boy like Reggie. Caught up in a conflicted and insecure world, threatened by losses all around him, Reggie's mind was doing precisely what it had been designed to do: protect him from the pain in his life. At 11 years of age, he hardly had the skills to survive by himself, and the fear of being abandoned by his parents was so intolerable that the only thing his mind could do was to anesthetize those feelings.

So gradually a depression had come over him. No actual loss had taken place, but he was surrounded by the threatened losses of his home, of one of his parents, of moving to another part of the country as his mother kept discussing, and of disruption to his whole life. What is a young child supposed to do when surrounded by such threats? The best protection the mind can devise is depression.

 As we fall into depression, and "fall" is a good description, we become lethargic, lose interest in normal activities, withdraw from people and our social environment, and then begin to wish we could escape this life. For Reggie, this depression, so early in his life, could easily become a lifelong pattern. In the future, whenever he is confronted by intense conflict or threatened losses, he will know what to do, because he has learned it so well as a child. This is perhaps the strongest argument for parents to get help for their children who are depressed. They need to learn healthier ways of coping with life's problems.

On the other hand, biological depressions are not as common in children as they are in adolescents or adults. As a child approaches puberty, however, important hormonal changes may affect mood and produce temporary depressions. By and large, however, younger children are not being pushed and pulled by their hormones. They are being tugged at by life itself and the experience of losses.

By far the most serious cause of childhood depression is the divorce or separation of parents; it's particularly damaging to a child approaching puberty. The divorce represents many losses, including the separation of the family, loss of one parent, and perhaps a change in environment with a loss of friends. There are also many threatened losses as the child anxiously tries to anticipate the future.

HOW DO FEELINGS OF FAILURE RELATE TO CHILDHOOD DEPRESSION?

Any experience of failure by a child can be the cause of depression because of the loss it represents. Not coping well at school, repeated failure, or an inability to perform at the same level as other children may seriously harm a child's self-image and self-esteem.

Parents who communicate extremely high standards to their children and the expectation that those standards be met may also be fostering a state of profound loss. Children who cannot live up to their parents' standards or who constantly feel rejected by parents because they're not "making it" may experience significant losses.

This is one of the reasons competition can be damaging to many children. Highly successful children thrive on competition. They win all the awards and get all the prizes, and that works wonders for their self-image and self-esteem. The problem is that only one person wins, and everyone else feels like a loser. I wish we had a system in our culture that would help *every* child to have a sense of being a winner, at least part of the time.

This is one reason I strongly advise parents to seek out activities for their children that naturally complement the children's talents. A child who isn't physically strong should not be pushed into a sport that requires great physical strength. An activity that naturally matches the child's abilities should be encouraged instead. This is also true in the academic realm. Some children are extremely gifted when it comes to using their hands, as in crafts, but may not be adept at mastering concepts out of books. Parents should value these other forms of intelligence and balance their expectations. I'll have more to say about this when I discuss the impact of depression on self-esteem at the end of this chapter.

In preparing children to cope with life, is it a good idea to put them in situations where they will fail so they'll learn to handle failure?

I don't believe so. We don't teach children to swim by throwing them into a swimming pool. Having a sound value system is far more important in coping with failure than the experience of failing. In fact, people who experience a lot of failure don't cope with defeat better than others; they cope less well and easily become depressed.

How can I best help my children cope with depression?

The most important thing is to open up communication. You must allow them the freedom to talk about their feelings of sadness. Don't be afraid to hear what they have to say. This can bring to light some significant factors in their environment that may be contributing to their depression, such as rejection or punishment by their peers, or difficulties at school. When you know what's causing the depression, you're in a better position to help.

One time a parent came to see me because her child was depressed and didn't want to go to school. The mother was blaming herself, thinking the problem was something she had done. I asked if she had talked to her daughter about it. No, she hadn't, because she thought that if she brought the matter into the open, it might aggravate her daughter's depression.

I encouraged her to talk to her daughter. The result was the discovery that her daughter was having trouble with another child in a physical education class. It had nothing to do with the mother. The girls exercised in shorts, and this girl was making fun of her legs. As soon as we identified the cause of the depression, the mother knew what to do. She talked to the school counselor, her daughter changed physical education classes, and the depression lifted.

You should also teach your children sound values. Early in life, they need to learn not to give too much worth to material things. That helps to minimize the growth of an exaggerated sense of loss over them.

It's important, too, that you build your children's self-respect and self-esteem. Help them to discover their strengths. Some children grow up believing they're no good at anything simply because their parents failed to encourage experimentation with a wide variety of interests. Encourage your kids to find something they can do well so that they can feel a sense of mastery and accomplishment about it.

Furthermore, teach your children how to delay gratification. By this I mean they should be taught that all their needs cannot be met immediately. Some rewards must wait. There's a tendency in our culture to expect to have our needs satisfied instantly. That sets us up for a lot of frustration and depression, because life just doesn't work that way. We must all learn to wait for life's prizes. After all, we don't get paid every minute as we work. We have to wait. Our gratification must be delayed.

Let me illustrate how I did this with my own children. In her earliest years, my youngest daughter tended to be impulsive in wanting her needs met. She'd ask me to do something for her or would want some money. I would respond gently, "Yes, as soon as I'm finished with what I'm doing, I'll get it for you." Initially she would have a little temper tantrum. I would patiently respond with, "As soon as I'm ready, I'll get it for you." I would wait a few minutes, then stop what I was doing and do as I had promised.

Soon she came to realize that I always kept my word, so she learned how to wait. But make sure you do follow through with what you've promised or you'll only create more frustration.

If you can introduce a bit of delay whenever it's reasonable and then follow through on what you've promised, you can help your children become more patient. Believe me, in later years that will help them to avoid a lot of depression.

Finally, reinforce as strongly as you possibly can God's love toward your child. The deep realization that one is loved and cared for by God can transcend feelings of depression and self-hate. Parents are imperfect, and there is no way we can command the same respect or create the same memory of perfect love in our children as God can. Most children can grasp the perfection of God's love and the unchanging nature of His caring. Teach your child about God, therefore, and point him or her to the experience of strength God can give. That will help your child to weather the present storm and to face the pressures of life in the future.

Because God loves us, He never forsakes us, even though many of our friends might. He stands with us, and when we reach the rock bottom of despair, we discover it is a solid rock that rises to the surface to sustain us. You may not be able to take away all the feelings of uselessness, but you can certainly help your child feel secure in the knowledge of God's love.

HOW CAN I TEACH MY CHILDREN TO GRIEVE THEIR LOSSES?

When we teach our children how to grieve their losses, they recover from them more quickly. We can begin in kindergarten to show them how losses are inevitable and what we should do about them. I vividly remember my grandmother helping me to grieve over the loss of a pet bird. It was a canary of a deep yellow hue. My grandmother kept it on the front porch, because it had such a beautiful song. Every time I visited her, I fed the bird and cleaned its cage. It became a special pet to me.

During one school vacation, while I was visiting, my grandfather got up early one morning to discover that the bird was dead in its cage. He tried to sneak it out so I wouldn't see it, but my grandmother stopped him. "Children must learn how to grieve also," she scolded. Then she promptly sat me down to explain that animals don't live as long as people and that for all of them, a time comes when they have to die. This is true for people also, she reminded me. We need to be brave, accept such losses, and get on with our lives.

She suggested I find a shoe box, line it with an old cloth, and make a coffin for the bird. Later that day, she said, "We'll have a little funeral service. This is our way of saying good-bye, and you'll feel better because of it."

She was absolutely right. At first I felt so overwhelmed by the death of that little bird that I wasn't sure I wanted to be a part of any funeral. By the time I had dug a little grave, said a prayer, and covered up the box with dirt, however, I began to feel relief and could accept the loss as something natural. Life would move on.

This is true of many of life's experiences. Not only do friends and loved ones, as well as pets, die, but childhood also passes away, children marry and leave home, friends abandon us, and eventually we grow old and decline in health. These losses are all inevitable, and the sooner we learn to detach ourselves from them, the sooner we will recover.

HOW COMMON IS ADOLESCENT DEPRESSION?

In contrast to the debate over whether depression exists in childhood, there has been little doubt about adolescent depression. We've known for a long time that adolescence is a period of extreme emotional discomfort; most of us have been through it ourselves.

While we have no clear statistics on the incidence of depression in adolescence, a study conducted in the Oregon Depression Project discovered that whereas at any one time about 3 percent of adolescents were significantly depressed, there was a one in five chance of any child's becoming depressed during the period of adolescence. The risk for girls was about twice that of boys, and treatment was highly recommended for 93 percent of those considered to be depressed.

With the growing frequency of adolescent suicide, many experts now believe it is far more common than in adulthood. In my opinion, at least one out of every two children will experience significant depression sometime during the adolescent period. At any one time, probably one out of five adolescents could be considered clinically depressed.

A significant finding of the Oregon Depression Project was that 43 percent of the teenagers diagnosed as depressed also had other mental disorders over their lifetime. Depression existed together with physical diseases, and when it occurred with another mental disorder, it was more likely to follow than precede that disorder.

Depressed teens were likely to be female and come from a one-parent family or not live with their natural parents. Grade at school, average size of household, number of siblings, and occupation of the head of the household made no difference. They were likely to have experienced stressful events within the recent past; to be pessimistic, turned inward, and have a negative body image and low self-esteem; to be emotionally dependent on others; to be self-conscious; and to report less social support than others. This means that for many of them, the only social support they could point to was their own family.

WHAT ARE THE SYMPTOMS OF ADOLESCENT DEPRESSION?

Because adolescence is a period of emotional upheaval anyway, depression may be hard to recognize. Feelings of sadness, loneliness, anxiety, and hopelessness that are normally associated with depression may also be seen in the normal stresses of growing up. Some adolescents who are depressed act out their distress, becoming inappropriately angry or aggressive, running away, or becoming delinquent. Such behaviors can easily be dismissed as "typical adolescent storminess," and their significance in pointing to the presence of a serious depression is overlooked. Any of these signs, therefore, should be examined closely in case they indicate depression.

In determining whether an adolescent is depressed, we have to look at what changes have taken place. The following questions may help to clarify the state of the adolescent mind:

- Has the once-outgoing child become withdrawn and antisocial as an adolescent?
- Was the adolescent formerly a good student but is now failing or skipping classes?
- Was the child happy-go-lucky but is now moping around for weeks or months?
- Is the teenager inappropriately irritable, whereas once he or she was calm and longsuffering?

If your answer is yes to any of these questions, it may indicate you need to get some help for your teenager. In addition, if your youngster feels unable to cope, demoralized, friendless, or is possibly suicidal, it's almost certain that he or she is depressed.

One of the complicating factors of adolescence is that bipolar disorder (also called manic-depressive illness) often emerges. This is a more serious form of depression, although it is perhaps the more easily treated. It is manifested by periods of impulsiveness, irritability, loss of control, and sometimes bizarre behavior when the teenager is unable to sleep and engages in a lot of meaningless but manic behavior. This is not just the normal ups and downs of adolescence. Rather, it is going from a period of intense hyperactivity, which may last for many months, into severe depression, and back again to normal. Such a disorder needs immediate professional treatment.

DOES ADOLESCENT DEPRESSION IN THIS COUNTRY DIFFER FROM THAT IN OTHER CULTURES?

In many cultures, adolescence is a period of significant mood disruption. Some cultures minimize these reactive depressions because they have much clearer "rituals of transition" from childhood to adulthood. In our culture, an adolescent must not only weather the storm of biological change, as in all cultures, but also the social and cultural storms of transition. Therefore, depression is much more of a problem here than in more-tribal cultures. Adolescence is probably the most difficult stage of life for any person in the Western world to negotiate. Most adults remember the pain of their adolescence vividly and with much regret.

It's common for adolescents to feel they're going crazy. No one understands them, so they must be the ones out of step with the world. Considerable emotional

distress is the norm rather than the exception, and it comes at a time of life when they're extremely vulnerable to stress. They have adult bodies but still only children's minds. Because of improvements in health and living conditions, we grow up faster these days physically, and we are almost fully developed and capable of being parents before we have the mental ability to take care of ourselves. The result is that there are many reasons for depression in adolescence, just as there are many causes for loss.

Alicia is typical of many adolescents. Once a happy child and a good student, she became depressed when she turned 14. She grew withdrawn, listless, and disinterested in school and her friends, except for one close friend she had known since she was a young child. She lost all her energy and enthusiasm. This was so noticeable because she had been energetic and enthusiastic about life. She developed a pervasive sadness that discouraged friendships with others and, except for her one close friend, became isolated.

Slowly she began to skip classes. Then, to avoid her mother's nagging, she started staying away from home until late in the evening. When she finally returned home, she feigned extreme tiredness and ran up to her bedroom, dropped on the bed, and pretended she was asleep. Alicia's mother became increasingly upset at her behavior.

Alicia's father was an alcoholic, so he hadn't paid much attention to what was going on. Often he came home late, drunk, and that left Alicia's mother to be the sole parenting figure in the home. Because she felt hopelessly inadequate, she consulted with her pastor, who, after a brief period of consulting, convinced her Alicia was suffering from a significant depression. He referred Alicia's mother to a psychiatrist, who finally admitted Alicia to an adolescent treatment program in the local hospital.

With some coercion from the psychiatrist, the father joined Alicia and her mother in family therapy, and the healing process began. However, healing would not have been completed without the help of some important medication.

It was clear to the psychiatrist that Alicia was suffering from a biological form of depression that was being aggravated by the unsatisfactory home conditions. Typical of many adolescent depressions is this interaction between biological and psychological or environmental factors. The one plays off the other. The biological deficiency reduces an adolescent's ability to cope with his or her home, school life, and peer conflicts, so a significant reactive depression becomes superimposed upon hormonal or other biological changes. Treatment is only effective if *both* factors are addressed.

Fortunately for Alicia, she was in competent hands, and recovery was rapid. I regret to say I have encountered many adolescents who are depressed and have not found the same level of professional competence, so their misery has been prolonged unnecessarily for years.

How can I get help for my child or teenager?

The first step in getting help is, of course, to get your child to acknowledge the depression. That isn't always easy. You may want to talk it over with your spouse, a close friend, or your pastor before you confront your child. Alternatively, take your child to your family physician, and have him or her explain the problem.

How you proceed after that depends on the age of the child. Young children are usually quite compliant. Taking them to a professional for help, provided you prepare the way adequately and don't intensify their anxiety, should not be a problem. Many psychologists and psychiatrists specialize in childhood disorders. They know how to talk to a child and how to make the experience pleasant. If you don't feel comfortable with the first professional you consult, move to someone else.

Specific treatments include various forms of play therapy, family therapy, and the use of antidepressants or other medications in the event that there is some biological complication.

What should I do if my child refuses help?

The older the child, the more difficult it may be to get appropriate help. A depressed 10- or 12-year-old may be quite resistant to going to see a professional, and you certainly cannot expect a child of that age to go alone. Make sure you or your spouse accompanies the child to provide a comforting source of reference.

Because the risk of suicide increases the older the child becomes and is particularly hazardous in the adolescent years, it's imperative that a depressed adolescent be seen by a mental health professional as soon as possible. A teenager may resist treatment, so it may be necessary for you, as a parent, to "get tough" or use some form of coercion.

In this regard, teenagers are extremely astute, even uncanny, in their ability to know if parents feel guilty or ambivalent about getting help for them. They can sense your indecisiveness, so you should, as parents, make up your minds what it is you want to do and then communicate an absolute sense of togetherness when it comes to telling your teenager you want him or her to get help.

Sometimes it's wise for parents to seek help for themselves before they approach their depressed child. If the youngster is destructive of self or others, it is essential that you don't delay. But if you can have an appointment yourself ahead of your child, you might find it easier to communicate firmness.

My daughter is so depressed that I'm afraid she's going to commit suicide. What should I do?

Many parents are left with severe guilt problems after their child has attempted or been successful in suicide. I've worked with several such parents, and I can assure you that those feelings cannot be dealt with easily. It is far better to get help, even if it's not absolutely necessary, than afterward to regret not having taken any action. You'll have a lot less guilt and pain to deal with if you've acted prematurely than if you have not acted at all.

If your teenager resists treatment, discuss this first with the mental health professional. He or she will advise you on how to get tough, particularly if the teenager is using alcohol or drugs and is getting into trouble. "Getting tough" doesn't mean physically or verbally abusing your child. It does mean not being intimidated by any threats of running away. You present a united and unmovable front—and force the child into treatment.

Getting tough also means seeing to it that your teenager follows through on treatment. If this becomes a problem, your treatment specialist may request that the child be hospitalized. This is particularly necessary if there is any threat to life. Your youngster may be better off in a psychiatric hospital, a drug rehabilitation program, or a residential treatment center, where the most intense forms of treatment can be provided.

Remember that a depressive disorder is not a passing bad mood but an illness that should and can be treated. This is not the time to be caught up with doubts or to allow inexperienced friends to give you advice that may sound spiritual but could be devastating if things go wrong. Adolescent depression is a serious disorder with serious consequences. Don't hesitate to get appropriate help. God will honor your actions and completely understands why you need to act with speed and firmness.

How does self-esteem relate to adolescent depression?

All forms of depression at all ages have a serious effect on self-esteem. Since the impact is greatest in childhood and adolescence, I want to discuss the topic briefly in this chapter.

Repeated depressions have a demoralizing effect. Each time one is depressed, one's sense of well-being, self-confidence, and self-image gradually erodes. After a little while and many depressions, this erosion becomes permanent, and the person comes to feel worthless.

I recall treating an adolescent over several years who suffered from frequent depressions. After the first bout, when he was only 14, he felt quite negative about himself. He also felt uncertain about whether he could cope with his life adequately. After that brief bout of depression, his confidence gradually came back, and within a period of three months, his feelings about himself had returned to normal.

Six months later, however, he went into another depression. We started the antidepressant medication immediately, but it was almost a month before the depression began to lift. By then he had become even more demoralized than the first time, and it took at least six months after his recovery before he began to feel confident and not too unsure of himself again.

One year later, a third depression hit, and this time he was so deeply affected that even though the depression itself lifted quickly, he continued to be in a state of intense self-depreciation. This required many months of ongoing psychotherapy to help him restore his diminished self-esteem.

What this illustrates is how depression affects self-esteem, not just during the depression, but afterward as well. It also emphasizes the importance of getting treatment for a child's or adolescent's depression as soon as possible. Untreated depression can be a major cause of low self-esteem later in life.

Depression undermines our sense of worth and distorts our self-image, which are the basis for self-esteem. While I don't like the term *self-esteem* because it can be so easily misunderstood as a form of self-adoration, no other term adequately captures the concept. We all have an attitude toward ourselves, a self-image or self-concept that is the "picture" we carry around in our mind's eye of who and what we are. We then place a value on this self-image, either positive or negative, which is what we call self-esteem.

I don't believe we should have "high" or "low" self-esteem, but simply that our esteem should be free of self-hate or self-rejection. "Low" self-esteem is a contradiction in terms. It really means self-hate, not esteem. The appropriate attitude toward oneself as a Christian should be self-transparency. We shouldn't be too concerned about how we feel toward ourselves, except that we should not be excessively self-rejecting or self-hating. Self-acceptance is the key to a healthy self-esteem, not self-adoration. If we've been accepted in Christ, we ought to value ourselves just as He does.

Frequent depressions cause self-doubt and self-depreciation. We develop a sense of being without worth, and that lies at the root of almost all personal, moral, and spiritual problems. Our actions are consistent with how we see and feel about ourselves, so it's important that those feelings be realistic. A child who is frequently depressed will grow up with a profound feeling of self-hate, which in turn will affect his or her life, marriage, present, and future. It also affects how we relate to God in later life. People with a lot of self-rejection find it difficult to really believe God has accepted them.

It's common, therefore, for people with low self-esteem to not only feel worthless, but also insecure. They feel rejected, as if they don't deserve friends. They're easily humiliated, which causes more depression that they use as a way of escaping from life. They become convinced that nobody likes them, and it is then easy to retreat into fantasy or to blame others for how they feel. This is one of the reasons adolescence is a period in which aimlessness, negativism, and finally drugs, alcoholism, suicide, and other self-defeating behaviors set in. In a sense, those behaviors become alternative ways of dealing with depression.

HOW CAN I HELP MY CHILDREN SURVIVE DEPRESSION WITHOUT DAMAGING THEIR SELF-ESTEEM?

There are essentially two strategies to follow. The *first* is a strategy of prevention, and the *second* is a strategy of recovery.

If you build your child's self-esteem on a solid footing of self-acceptance, you can prevent or minimize a loss of self-esteem in the event that a depression should strike. Children brought up in an atmosphere of acceptance, love, praise for legitimate achievements, and affirmation, and who have a strong feeling of possessing a "place of belonging" with relatives, friends, and peers, never really suffer from self-hate. Such children are "inoculated" against depression's devastating effects on self-esteem.

On the other hand, children who are frequently criticized, rejected, misunderstood, or labeled as stupid, clumsy, fat, or bad will always feel left out. Whenever they experience depression, the first part of the self that will be attacked is the esteem. Depression only convinces them that they are bad, inadequate, and failures. It reinforces the self-hate so easily triggered during times of depression. These children begin to think there is something wrong with them. They're not as important as others. They don't really belong. They are disappointments or even misfits and have nothing to offer. Such children often end up with the attitude "I wish I were dead."

Prevention is, therefore, best achieved by building your child's sense of worth and by doing it honestly, recognizing we all fall short of God's standards and that there's a sense in which we are all unworthy before God. However, God has loved us enough to die for us, and that means we *do* have value in His sight.

On the one hand, we need to teach our children where they stand in their relationship to God and their need of His salvation. But that doesn't mean we have to teach them they're unworthy or totally undeserving of His affection. It is *not* our task to reject and punish our children for their sinfulness. God will speak to their consciences. Our job is to teach them how to respect themselves, despite their sinfulness, so they can come to know God fully and receive His forgiveness. This is a tightrope we walk as parents, but unless we get it right, we won't give our children the skills and self-attitudes they need to weather the storms of depression.

Parents should not be short on praise, only on criticism. We need to modify our expectations so our children can have a sense of accomplishment. They need to feel free to express themselves and to believe their parents take them seriously. No parent should demand performance from a child that cannot reasonably be met. That only reinforces a sense of failure and self-rejection. Through acceptance, affection, and approval, parents can build a secure and adequate self-image upon which a healthy sense of self can develop.

This sense of personal worth becomes even more precious when children feel accepted by God and receive the gift of Christ's dying on their behalf. They then enjoy that deep and abiding sense of forgiveness and assurance that God is helping them to grow into more-complete human beings.

How can I help my child recover his self-esteem?

Prevention is only the first strategy. The second is one of helping a child recover from low self-esteem. Even if we build a solid base of prevention, there are times when we must help a child rebuild lost esteem. Some depressions are so severe that no matter how solid a shield children have built for themselves in terms of their self-image, their depression will undermine their self-esteem. They doubt God, they doubt themselves, and they quickly move to a place of self-hate.

Recovery is best achieved by the same steps as prevention. We seek to reinforce feelings of acceptance, approval, and validation. We take our children back to the cross, where they can claim forgiveness for any sins that have been affecting them. Then, having claimed this forgiveness, they can move forward (see Phil. 3:13).

Try to help your depressed child to not live in the past but to look to the future; to not wallow in failure but to rise up in hope. By helping your child accept that there are reasons for the depression, you can minimize self-rejection or self-blame. The more children understand about the nature of their depression, the more they will be able to contain its negative effects.

Keep affirming the potential of your child. It can be very helpful to give a letter to your child during times of depression, expressing your affirmation and love in written form. Such a letter can become a prized possession. I know one adult who received such a letter from his parents when he was in a deep depression as an adolescent, and he keeps the letter in his Bible as a constant reminder that he is deeply loved. Whenever he feels depressed, he reminds himself of the depth of his parents' love. That's especially precious to him, because both his parents have now gone to be with the Lord.

It can also be helpful to show children how to focus outwardly and not be so preoccupied with their inner feelings. In other words, try to help children to focus less on themselves and more on others. Suggest projects that can serve others, such as writing a letter to some elderly relative or, if they're old enough, volunteering at a charitable organization or simply visiting some elderly person in their neighborhood. It's amazing how this helps to restore a child's (or anyone's, for that matter) sense of value. Serving others is always rewarded by feeling better about yourself.

Section II

Healing Your Depression

Many of the questions I have tried to answer in section I touch on issues of healing. While they stand by themselves and are helpful to someone struggling with depression, they do not by themselves provide a systematic overview of the healing process.

In this section I would like to bring these healing principles together and take the reader through a step-by-step process to show how healing from depression can be achieved.

The focus in this section deals with what you can do to cope with depression, how professional treatment works, and what you can do to help your depressed friends and family members. If you're depressed, use this information as you discuss problems and insights with a concerned friend or counselor. If your depression is in the past, you'll be sharply aware of the value of this material. The insights given will help prepare you to avoid much depression in the future and to modify the intensity of depression that is unavoidable.

F I V E

Coping with Depression
Part 1

To *cope*, according to the dictionary, means "to engage in a contest or battle on even terms or with success." One of the problems in coping, however, arises when we face a battle sorely hindered by inadequate weapons. Misinformation, no information, an inadequate understanding of the adversary—all weaken our position and assure the struggle will be long and painful.

Nowhere is this more true than in coping with depression. Whereas in many confrontations our weapons and strategies are developed and sharpened in the battle itself, the nature of depression is such that it dampens our energies in those directions. A mild depression may motivate us to generate ways of resolving it, but the deeper depressions seem to suck all ambition from us and leave us with a growing difficulty in maintaining any sense of perspective on our problem.

Fortunately, there is much you can do—ways you can contend with most depressions that will lessen their severity and shorten their duration. I'll be describing these in this and the next chapter.

IS THERE SOME FORMULA I CAN FOLLOW TO OVERCOME DEPRESSION?

There's no easy prescription. In one sense, no two depressions are identical, and no two people experience depression the same way. Yet there are fundamental principles that should be followed; I've touched on some of them already.

The "formula" must be tailored to the type of depression you experience. If you get depressed regularly without any apparent cause, the first step is to get a good medical evaluation and try to discover if there's a physical cause for your depression. If there is, have the depression taken care of with appropriate treatment.

If the depression is reactive, caused by a loss of some sort, there are several things you can do.

First, let me say again, if it's a minor depression, don't do anything. Just accept it and allow yourself to go through it. You may well realize what's causing it. Minor depressions are usually self-healing provided you don't feed them with too much introspection.

If, however, you feel your depression is more serious, try the following steps:

Step 1: Identify the loss with all its implications.
Step 2: Accept the loss, do your grieving, and try to put the loss in some perspective.
Step 3: Then get on with your life.

Of these three steps, identifying and understanding your loss is the most difficult. Sometimes the loss is very subtle or abstract, making it hard—even impossible—to identify. Or you may be so depressed that it's tough to do this sort of self-searching. In that case, I suggest you talk with somebody you feel can be understanding and nonjudgmental, perhaps a friend or your spouse. Just discussing your depression with someone else may help you to see what's causing it. If that doesn't help and the depression lasts for several days or weeks, seek further help from your pastor, a counselor, or a psychologist.

Identifying the loss isn't always necessary, however. Many depressions burn themselves out if we remain patient. Fortunately, our brains are designed to forget, so much that bothers us gets washed away with the passage of time. But if you find yourself unable to come out of the depression, you need to seek professional help.

Suppose you lose your job. For economic reasons, the company lets you go. You become depressed. That's natural. (If you didn't become depressed, I'd be concerned.) If the depression lasts even a couple of weeks, that's probably not significant. You'll get over it as soon as you pull your life together. However, if you not only lose your job but also have difficulty finding another, your depression may intensify to the point where you need help. It may be so severe that you can't do what's necessary to get another job.

How do I deal with the loss after I've identified it?

It's often difficult to understand the full implications of a loss. Some losses are so subtle that you need someone like a therapist to help you understand their full meaning. The next step is to move to an acceptance of the loss. You must stop fighting or resenting it. You can't go on wishing the thing you've lost will come back. This acceptance is an act of your will, a conscious decision in your mind. The grief process, allowing yourself to become sad, helps this.

The last step often goes hand in hand with acceptance, or it may follow it. You must pull back and put the loss in some larger perspective so it does not continue to dominate your life. As a Christian, you must begin to see the loss from God's point of view. Some of the things we grieve over are rather insignificant when we put them in the context of the larger scheme of things. Having a clear plan and purpose for your life, with a deep understanding that God is in control, can help you accept and put losses in perspective more easily than if you lack such beliefs.

What is the role of anger in depression?

Anger and depression often coexist, but the notion that depression is anger turned inward is a misunderstanding of the relationship between the two. The loss that causes a depression often simultaneously causes a feeling of frustration. And when we're frustrated, we become angry. The anger is designed to help overcome our frustration. This is then interpreted as the anger "turned inward."

So it would be wrong to suggest in most cases that anger is a trigger mechanism in depression?

Anger may be the trigger mechanism in some cases, but it usually occurs simultaneously with the depression in reaction to a common loss. In rare cases, depression may occur without anger, but usually the loss triggers both. People suppress the anger in some depressions.

Perhaps the best example of this is in bereavement. You can't be angry at the person who just died, so you don't allow your anger to surface. Often, as I help people through the grief process, a large part of the counseling is focused on getting them in touch with this anger. It may be directed at the hospital, at the doctors, at fate, or even at God. Sometimes there is anger at the deceased for abandoning them. Identifying and dealing with this anger is essential in resolving the depression.

WILL ANGER FUEL A DEPRESSION SPIRAL?

Anger easily creates other emotions, and it can fuel a spiral in which a depression keeps getting worse. You're not only angry at the loss, but you're angry at yourself for being depressed.

Because many have been taught that depression is wrong, they feel guilty about being depressed. This in turn makes them angry at themselves for not being able to shake off the depression. The anger represents further loss—the loss of self-esteem for being unable to control their emotions—which perpetuates and intensifies the depression. They find themselves in a spiral: more depression followed by more anger, which causes deeper depression. Soon they feel as if there is no way out.

HOW CAN I HANDLE MY ANGER IN A HEALTHY WAY?

Dealing with anger is just as complex and difficult as dealing with depression. Briefly, though, handling anger involves three steps. First, you must recognize and own the feeling of anger. For many people, anger goes unnoticed or is denied. They will sit there, livid in the face, breathing hard. But if you say to them, "Oh, you're angry," they'll immediately answer, "Angry? I'm not angry!" and nearly bite your head off.

My strong conviction, based on scriptural principles, is that the *feeling* of anger is legitimate. What you *do* with your anger (the aggressive behavior), however, may not be. The feeling is a symptom that something is wrong— something is hurting or frustrating you. But taking that anger out on somebody else—attacking the object of your anger—is wrong. Angry behavior has more potential for sin than just the feeling.

If you can admit your anger and use it to direct you back to what's causing it, you'll be in a better position to dispose of the anger. Unfortunately, we tend to want to savor the emotion. We want to feel hurt. And that, of course, contributes to depression.

Once you identify the cause of your anger, whether it's something someone else has done or something you did yourself, you can take the next step to resolving it: go to the person who is hurting or offending you and deal with the issue.

Resolution occurs when you come to terms with whatever is causing the anger.

All of us would benefit greatly by dealing with our anger causers in our "sane" moments. We often get angry at the same things over and again. Our spouses or our children do the same things repeatedly, and we get angry every time. For example, sometimes we have too-high expectations that are never met, causing frustration and anger. In our calm moments, we can reduce our anger by evaluating our expectations and making sure they're not unreasonable.

MUST A PERSON ALWAYS EXPRESS ANGER TO AVOID A DEPRESSION?

I strongly oppose the popular notion that you should always express anger at the time you feel it. Certainly you should be aware of your anger and strive hard to understand yourself and your emotions. But expressing your anger through angry behavior almost always creates more problems than it solves. It usually means you attack others and hurt feelings. They, then, have a need to hurt you back, and the process has no satisfactory ending.

I would distinguish, however, between aggressive expression of anger and simply saying to somebody, "I feel angry right now. I take responsibility for my anger, but I want to talk about it." The latter is healthy. It helps you to get a perspective on what's causing your anger. It also helps you to better understand why you're depressed.

The translation of anger as feeling into anger as aggression is where we have the greatest potential for sin. To act out your anger risks hurting others. Aggression is simply a way of getting revenge on those who cause your anger.

In summary, it's not necessary to act out your anger, but it is necessary to be in touch with it—to recognize it, to be able to label it accurately, and even to talk about it. You must accept the anger as your own. No one forces you to be angry. You bring it on yourself. Use it as a means of understanding your loss and helping you to put the loss in better perspective.

IF THE PHYSIOLOGICAL REACTIONS IN ANGER ARE BEYOND MY CONTROL, HOW CAN I BECOME LESS ANGRY WITHOUT REPRESSING THE EMOTION?

Physiological reactions to anger are beyond your control, but the anger itself is fueled and controlled by thoughts. If you put yourself in a pattern of resenting your loss, your physiology is going to follow that pattern. So while you can't stop your physiology, you can change your thinking. If you put your loss in perspective and deal with the hurt, your physiology will react in a different way. Remember that feelings are a product of a complex exchange between your mind and your body. Your thinking can cause your body to react in certain ways.

This is why the Christian gospel is so wonderful in helping you achieve mental health. It gives you fantastic resources. I'm thinking particularly of the gift of forgiveness, which can release you from a lot of anger.

Much of what causes anger can be handled internally without ever having to express it outwardly. Mind you, this is only true if you're able to understand your anger. (More about this later.)

CAN I AVOID SELF-HATE DURING A DEPRESSION?

The self-hate that occurs in a depression is part of the depression itself. The best way to deal with it is to be aware that it's one of the symptoms. In other words, the self-hate is so intimately bound up with your depression that you can't really avoid it. To get rid of it would be like getting rid of the depression itself. If you can recognize this and accept it as part of your depression at the time, you can avoid giving it too much attention. You're better off ignoring it.

This is an important principle in dealing with many negative emotions. Numerous feelings can't be avoided. But an emotion doesn't have to control you. You simply set it to one side. You say to yourself, *I realize this feeling is part of my depression, so I'm not going to give it any attention. I'm not going to respond to this false signal.* It takes some willpower, but it can be done.

HOW IS GUILT RELATED TO THE DEPRESSION SPIRAL?

Guilt feelings may be associated with the loss itself, especially if you see yourself as contributing to the cause of the loss. More frequently, though, guilt feelings arise because you think you should not be depressed. The guilt is caused by rejecting the right to be depressed. This guilt represents further loss, of course, the loss of self-respect. It adds to, and may be more significant than, the original loss.

Let's say you slam a door because you're angry, and it falls off its hinges. You're confronted with a concrete loss. You'll have to pay to fix the door. That loss would probably cause a mild depression even in the absence of any other emotion. But reacting to what you've just done, you begin to feel guilty. You sense a loss of respect for yourself because you're so quick-tempered. The guilt creates further loss that's probably larger than the original loss. So it produces a deeper depression that masks the earlier one. The guilt then feeds your depression with further loss and further depression, creating a depression spiral.

IS THERE A DIFFERENCE BETWEEN REAL AND FALSE GUILT?

Yes, there's an important difference. Some actions *should* make us feel guilty, such as failure to pay our debts or deliberately hurting others. That's real, legitimate guilt arising out of our responsibility for some wrong. It has a basis in reality.

False guilt, however, has no basis in reality. It's a tendency to internalize arbitrary rules and principles. Often they're instilled by parents, although they may be picked up from many other sources as well.

Let's say, for example, that your parents taught you to place your knife and fork at a certain angle on the plate when you finish eating. That was the "right" thing to do. Years later, as an adult, you have internalized that rule to such an extent that if your plate is taken from you before you can adjust the knife and fork to the correct angle, you feel extremely guilty. That's false guilt.

Sometimes it's called neurotic guilt. You're being controlled by an extremely arbitrary set of rules and values. They're not moral absolutes but a set of human quirks. Many of us are full of these petty rules. They should be confronted, their power to control you challenged.

HOW CAN I FORGIVE MYSELF FOR MY PAST FAILURES?

The tendency not to forgive ourselves is common in our culture. It seems to be related to the amount of false guilt we generate. Its roots are in early childhood, when parents fail to demonstrate forgiveness to their children, who keep on punishing themselves even as adults.

Self-forgiveness starts by accepting God's forgiveness in Christ and really letting that get down into the deepest part of your being. You have to believe Christ died for you and that God's forgiveness is for *all* your faults.

HOW CAN I DEAL WITH THE GUILT I FEEL ABOUT THE WAY MY DEPRESSION IS AFFECTING MY SPOUSE?

The first thing to do is to be open with your spouse about how you feel. We often walk around feeling guilty because we don't check things out. Since we don't talk it over, we get into the trap of imagining lots of things that may not be true at all. But even if your family is feeling bad because you're depressed, it's important to talk about it so they understand where you're coming from and you understand what they're feeling. Even if they're genuinely hurting, that's no reason for you to feel guilty. Don't allow your guilt to feed the depression or to create further negative emotions that could feed it.

How can we avoid depressions that appear to be related to helplessness?

People in our culture tend to feel helpless when they're manipulated by circumstances. They feel control is beyond them, so they don't try to take control of their lives. We call this "learned helplessness." If you regularly give control to others—a spouse, parents, church officials—you will often find yourself in depression.

You need to find ways to take control of your life. This requires some assertiveness, a characteristic usually lacking in those who frequently feel helpless. And people who are not as assertive as they should be, who can't or won't stand up for their rights, will often become depressed. So, very simply, the answer is to begin taking control of your circumstances.

Can a person who feels good about himself ever become depressed?

Absolutely. Feeling good about yourself doesn't prevent depression because, again, depression is a natural and normal reaction to loss, which we all experience. However, feeling good about yourself because you're in Christ and know He is doing His work in you does help to put losses in perspective and so resolve your grief more effectively.

How is self-pity related to depression?

Self-pity is also one of the by-products or symptoms of depression. Depression not only makes the world look bleak, but it makes you look bleak as well, so you tend to feel sorry for yourself. Self-pity gives rise to the aspect of depression known as *melancholia*, the tendency to feel very, very sad. Nothing seems worthwhile, especially yourself. As with the other negative emotions that accompany depression, self-pity can deepen the depression by adding further losses to the original one. This cycle must be broken to prevent the depression from deepening.

How do I deal with depression that seems to be related to an inadequate self-image?

The depressions having to do with one's self-image are the result of very subtle losses. They're difficult to get a handle on. To deal effectively with them, you have to work at it in your "sane" moments. You can't do this sort of work while you're depressed, because there is usually a lot of irrational thinking associated with it.

Building self-esteem involves two steps, the first of which is *self-understanding*. Often low self-esteem stems from a childhood that has created an erroneous self-image. Perhaps the parents used put-downs excessively, expressions like "You're dumb." "You'll never amount to anything." "You really disappoint me!" Coming from people who had a lot of power in their lives, such critical statements produce a distorted self-image. Although the statements may have been made in anger, they were made by people who were trusted and who should have shown love. Because of that, they were especially damaging.

It's vital that those early self-images be explored. The amazing thing is that *most* of us have a totally erroneous and negative view of ourselves. With help, we can correct those distortions and come to realize we're not nearly as bad as we believed.

The second step is *self-acceptance*. This is where being a Christian is so important. In Christ we have the whole basis for our self-acceptance. Whether we're better than we think we are or even worse, we can, through Christ's acceptance of us, move into accepting ourselves.

What's the difference between accepting myself and excusing myself?

This is an important distinction to make. Excusing yourself involves a lot of rationalizing, such as: "The reason I didn't perform well was that my grandmother was dying." That's not realistic self-knowledge but making an excuse for your behavior. Accepting yourself is having the courage to face both your strengths and your weaknesses and accept what you see. You may need to ask others to help you understand yourself. Then be honest enough to look at yourself from their point of view.

How can I have confidence in myself when everything I do seems to turn out wrong?

I'm sure most of us at one time or another have lacked confidence because everything seemed to be going wrong. One event after another seemed to collide with us in a destructive way. While this may occur due to an unfortunate series of circumstances over which we have no control, it may also be because we're not functioning maturely. We make bad decisions, so it's not surprising that things go wrong.

In those cases, it's a good idea to get some help. Maybe you need to understand yourself better. Maybe you're "blowing" things constantly because you have no understanding of what causes you to do what you do. I suggest you find professional help or at least talk things over with your pastor or a close friend.

HOW CAN I LOOK TO THE FUTURE WHEN MY PAST HAS BEEN SO DISMAL?

Many people have a deep-seated fear of the future because of the frequent and painful depressions they've experienced in the past. Often they have an endogenous form of depression. Medication or other medical treatment may be needed to restore the biochemical balance and thus assure the sufferer of a more-hopeful future.

If the frequent depressions are reactive, you're going to have to do some work within yourself to reduce your sense of hopelessness about the future. It may require you to make changes in how you cope with life. Improving how you handle stress could probably cut by half the depressions you experience. Even if the depression is legitimate and caused by a loss you can't control, better stress management increases your coping ability.

You need, then, to work on yourself, to improve your tolerance for stress and frustration. It's tragic to realize how many Christians are lethargic in this area, believing it will all take care of itself or that God will magically make everything right.

WHY DO I FEEL WORTHLESS EVEN THOUGH I KNOW I'M INTELLIGENT?

This is what depression does to our rational processes. Emotions, once triggered, are much more powerful in determining our actions than our intelligence or our reasoning. Depression is a deep emotion that interferes with our thinking process. Our rational abilities just get set aside as we focus on the emotion we're experiencing at the moment.

HOW CAN I COPE WITH FEELINGS OF INFERIORITY AND WORTHLESSNESS?

Feelings of inferiority and worthlessness form a cycle. They follow the depression, but they also feed it, thus keeping it going. Reacting to the depression with guilt, anger, or some other emotion gives the depression cycle extra momentum. That puts you into an ever-deepening depression. Somewhere you have to break the cycle by realizing that your feelings are part of the depression.

For example, if you haven't slept all night and the next morning you find you can't do your work properly, you don't need to go far to find the reason. So you don't punish yourself for your lack of effectiveness. You ask to be excused, and you go home and sleep. That's how you take care of such a problem. It's also how you should deal with your feelings of worthlessness and inferiority. Recognize that they're a consequence of your depression, and focus on dealing with the depression itself rather than letting the feelings add to the depression.

HOW CAN I SET REALISTIC GOALS FOR MYSELF IN THE CONTEXT OF PURSUING CHRISTLIKENESS?

Conformity to Christ, as I see it, is a direction in which we move. Paul himself said he was striving for that conformity, and yet I'm sure he knew that on this side of the grave he would never fully attain it. I'm suspicious of people who say they *are* Christlike, but I understand those who say they *want* to be Christlike. There's an important distinction between the two.

Having the desire to be Christlike doesn't mean you rule out the possibility of having a reactive depression. There will be losses, and you'll find yourself grieving these losses through your depression.

Further, when you set goals within the context of this direction, they need to be realistic. It's not realistic to have a mind-set that you must never be depressed. You should strive to minimize the impact of losses, however, especially materialistic ones, as you come to understand the mind of Christ.

Another important element here is that you need to develop a healthy "theology of failure." Some people's theology won't allow them to think in terms of failure. They only see God in their successes. But we are human beings simply striving to be Christlike. We will fail.

Satan uses failure more destructively than he should be able to because we don't know how to receive it from the hand of God. We need to see failures as stepping stones to growth. They are "to grow by." I'm not suggesting you should encourage failure so you can grow, but when failure does occur—when you fail to reach a goal you've set for yourself—you must consider setting more-realistic goals (if that's a problem), and you must make sure that feeling of failure does not become destructive.

IS IT TRUE THAT DEPRESSED PEOPLE SEEK RATIONALIZATIONS MORE THAN SOLUTIONS?

Since the purpose of depression is to remove people from the race, there's a loss of energy, of drive and ambition. There's also a tendency, therefore, to feel helpless and not to seek solutions. Depressed people often retreat into rationalization as a way of justifying their failure to do anything.

I recall a patient who was in a severe depression and as a consequence could not do his work properly. Instead of finding solutions, he sat there giving me elaborate explanations for why he couldn't get his work done. When I pressed him to write out four or five action steps that would help him be productive, he resisted strongly. Such resistance is a natural result of the depression. One just lacks the energy and drive to be action oriented.

TO WHAT EXTENT SHOULD A DEPRESSED PERSON TAKE RESPONSIBILITY FOR THE DEPRESSION?

You don't need to take responsibility for a depression before you can resolve it. The depression itself doesn't restore the loss. But you do have to take responsibility for dealing with the depression. It's probably not easy to do at the deepest time of your depression, but as you begin to "bottom out" and put the loss in perspective, you're responsible to deal with the consequences of the loss.

For instance, if you have lost your job, sooner or later you're going to have to do something about finding another. A time comes in the experience of depression when your energy starts to return and you can speed up your recovery by taking action.

IS THERE A TIME IN DEPRESSION WHEN IT'S IMPOSSIBLE TO HELP YOURSELF?

In some depressions (the less-severe ones), you can help yourself right through the depression. You're not that incapacitated. In the deeper depressions, however, there is a time early in the experience when it's impossible to help yourself. During that time, the best thing you can do is to remove yourself from your environment. Take some time off to be alone and allow yourself to do your grieving. Some depressives are afraid to do this because they're afraid they'll lose control if they give up, but it's the best thing to do when you're really low.

IS THERE A POSSIBILITY THAT "GIVING IN" TO YOUR DEPRESSION WILL FURTHER DEEPEN IT?

What will deepen a depression is to resist it, at least in the common, reactive depressions. When you experience a significant loss, you need a period of grieving. It may take a day or two, perhaps even a week or two or much longer, but it takes time. There comes a time when your energy begins to return, however. At that point, if you just get on that wave, you can speed up your recovery.

I must qualify this answer by stressing that I'm talking about the common, reactive depressions. If your depression is endogenous, it doesn't help to "give in" to it; that will only perpetuate it. Because it has its cause in the body's biochemical system, that balance must be restored before healing can occur. Withdrawing and giving in to this type of depression will not help. You should do whatever you can to minimize the impact of this depression.

Sometimes it helps to say to yourself, "Look. Cheer up. This is going to be over soon." Then go on about your normal routine. By talking to yourself this way, you can help to put your depression in better perspective. But avoid any self-talk that robs you of the right to be depressed; it will only aggravate the depression.

WHAT ARE THE KEY SCRIPTURAL PRINCIPLES INVOLVED IN COPING EFFECTIVELY WITH DEPRESSION?

I am assuming the reader understands and accepts that there must be a basic foundation of salvation in Christ and the indwelling power of the Holy Spirit. Beyond that, there are at least three scriptural principles I have found tremendously helpful.

First, both loss and gain are part of our Christian experience. We should not expect everything to be gain.

In Philippians 3:7-8, Paul said that the things that were once gain to him, he now counted as loss for Christ. He meant there is no loss we can experience that exceeds what we gain in Christ. He also said, in effect, "Everything I'm going to lose in the future, I will contrast with what I gain in Jesus Christ. That will help me to bear the loss and get over my grieving more quickly."

The principle of seeing what we gain in Christ can revolutionize our value systems. It can help us put our losses, whatever they are, in the perspective of eternity.

That doesn't mean depression won't bother us in the future. Even though Paul said he counted all his losses as gains, I don't think he was implying he never felt sorrow over some particular loss. It's a process, something we call to remembrance every day to help us cope with the losses of life. In fact, it's a healthy spiritual exercise to begin each day by taking all the losses you anticipate and, in advance, offsetting them by reminding yourself of your gains in Christ.

Second, we are called to forgive those who hurt us.

The principle of forgiveness is stated most clearly in the Sermon on the Mount (see Matt. 6:14-15). I cannot stress strongly enough how much I feel that many of our depressions are the by-product of our inability or unwillingness to forgive. We don't seem to be, by nature, very willing to do it. We prefer taking revenge. We harbor grudges. We savor resentments. Since most losses in life come to us at the hand of some other person, the principle of forgiveness is absolutely essential to the avoidance and healing of depression.

Third, we're instructed to "renew our minds."

As a Christian psychologist, I greatly appreciate Romans 12:2. Paul reminded us there that we are to be "transformed by the renewing" of our minds. Not only does that verse legitimate some of the things I try to do professionally, but it's also a broad concept essential to coping with depression. Part of what God offers us in Christ is a renewed mind. That includes a new way of thinking, new values, new beliefs, and new attitudes. All are necessary if we're to cope with depression in a healthy way.

WHAT UNIQUE RESOURCES DO WE HAVE AS CHRISTIANS IN COUNTERING DEPRESSION?

God gives us a fantastic supply of resources in the gospel. He not only gives us His power directly through the indwelling Holy Spirit, but He also gives us the resources of His Word and prayer. All of these are directly beneficial in dealing with our depressions.

One of the most direct benefits these resources provide is a unique perspective on this life, especially that it's temporary and transitional. We are just "passing through," as the spiritual says. This perspective gives us a set of values that greatly help us cope with depression, because they change our perception of what is and isn't loss.

Christianity also teaches us not to be attached to the things of this world.

The first step in the process of healing, therefore, is really a spiritual exercise. We need to examine our hearts periodically to determine the extent of our attachments to our jobs, our families, our loved ones, our reputations, our ambitions, our dreams, and even ourselves. Too many of us leave those attachments unexamined, and an unexamined life is an unhappy life. Then, with God's help, we can reorder them so they're within the normal bounds of attachment.

Let me give you a concrete example. I love my family very much. At times I honestly believe I'm overattached to each of them. Whenever I realize that, I ask for God's help to put my relationship with them in a more balanced place. I honestly acknowledge my overattachment, and then, by reflecting on His role in my life, I realize He is the only one to whom I should be "overattached." This slowly brings my feelings under control and allows my love for my family to be put into better perspective.

Such periodic readjusting of attachments can also help us in preparing to face the losses that will eventually occur with even the most precious of the persons or objects we have.

ARE THERE STAGES IN THE PROCESS OF RESOLVING DEPRESSION?

Yes, there are three: protest, despair, and detachment. These stages are similar for all forms of loss. As we examine our spiritual resources for dealing with depression, it will be helpful to tie them in to each stage.

The first stage is *protest*. This occurs when we discover a loss has occurred. It's the natural reaction of our minds and bodies and is probably designed to help us overcome the loss. When the young wife hears her husband is leaving her, she immediately begins to protest, even deny it. That mobilizes her to deal with the threat, and in some instances it may even help to prevent the loss from occurring. For most of us, however, the protest phase doesn't help at all. It makes us angry and often intensifies the pain we experience over the loss.

How can God help us in this protest stage? Christians I've tried to help through it tend to blame God, themselves, and anyone else who might get in the way. There's a high level of hostility, and it's even possible that they will try to take their own lives or harm the people responsible for their losses.

Recently there has been a spate of reports in the news of men who were fired from their jobs and returned within a day or two to take revenge on their fellow workers and those responsible for their dismissal. This is the protest stage of depression. It can be traumatic for some. But for most of us, who only have to deal with ordinary losses and separations, the protest stage may go no further than a high level of irritability and aggravation.

It's extremely difficult at this stage to implement spiritual disciplines such as prayer and scripture reading. However, every effort should be made to focus back on God as being in control of our lives and to avoid feeling totally helpless. Scripture verses can provide a solid foundation. We can focus on the greatness of God (e.g., Ps. 77:13; 95:3; 104:1) or on His power (e.g., 1 Chron. 29:12; 2 Chron. 25:8; Ps. 65:6; Rom. 16:25). We can also focus on the strength God makes available to His children (e.g., 2 Sam. 22:40; Isa. 40:31; 41:10; Eph. 3:16), or on the theme of endurance (e.g., 2 Tim. 2:3-4; 4:5; Heb. 12:6-8; James 1:12).

Scripture can also be extremely important in helping us control feelings of hostility toward those who may be causing our loss. Above all else, we must pray for the strength and courage to forgive those who might be responsible for what we're feeling. We also have to forgive ourselves for what we've done and how we're reacting. Scriptural verses about forgiveness can help to focus our minds and energy on more-constructive actions (e.g., Ps. 103:10-12; 130:3-4; Col. 1:12-13; 1 John 1:9).

During this protest stage, there's also a deep sense of injury and a groping to hold on to the lost object. Particularly in cases where the separation was not expected, there can be an exaggerated cry of alarm, panic, protest, and anger. God can help us with each of those reactions.

The task we have to accomplish during this stage is to become fully aware of the loss and not engage in denial. We must face up to the pain. The more effectively we can do that, the quicker will be our recovery. We may find we lack interest in establishing an attachment to a new object. In some cases, we might run out and try to replace the object as quickly as possible.

Sadly, this often happens in divorce situations, where the one who was rejected almost immediately searches for another partner. This is done for several reasons, including the need to punish the one who has walked away or to replace the loss so there is less sense of abandonment.

Obviously, lots of mistakes can be made in this stage, so we need to ask God to keep our minds focused on the grieving process and not allow us to rush out and do something foolish. *Grief never works itself out through substitution.* We can't just replace our losses. If we do, we may find ourselves with a delayed grief response at a later time in life.

WHAT IS THE DESPAIR STAGE?

The protest stage finally gives way to the second stage in the grieving process, *despair*. As soon as our losses or separations become realistic to us, the depression may intensify. In this despair, we lose interest in all other people or things. We want to hibernate and not be disturbed, and we become silent and sullen. We need our space; we need to be feeling our sadness and reflecting upon our loss.

During this stage, the real work of healing begins. And it's here that we need to turn to God and be renewed in our spirits. We cannot find comfort in people that is as enduring or meaningful as the comfort that comes from God. The theme of comfort, therefore, may be very helpful to those in the despairing stage of depression. They might appreciate such passages as Psalm 23, 2 Corinthians 1:3-4, Philippians 2:1, and 1 Thessalonians 4:18.

During this period, however, it's extremely difficult to strengthen or even maintain our spiritual lives. But we can take comfort in the fact that this is the work of the Holy Spirit and that God can maintain our spiritual lives without much effort or motivation from us. If we live in total surrender and dependence on the Holy Spirit, we can trust Him to heal our infirmities and strengthen our spirits even though we may not be very cooperative (see Matt. 9:28-29; Eph. 3:20; Phil. 1:6; 2 Tim. 1:12).

If you're a friend or loved one of others who are in the despair stage of depression, don't talk too much, but focus on listening. Read Scripture to them without judging or condemning, and pray for them, because they most likely won't be able to pray for themselves. You can be extremely helpful in putting into words what they feel, even though they're not able to muster the strength or interest to do it for themselves. (For more on how to help a friend, see chapter 9.)

HOW DO WE REACH THE FINAL STAGE OF DETACHMENT?

We discussed the importance of attachments in our lives in chapter 2. Let me add a few thoughts.

In every circumstance of loss or separation, the final goal of healing is to be no longer attached to the lost object but to become nonattached. This is the final stage of letting go.

Let's say you were released from your job and that even though you now have a new job, it's not as prestigious or as satisfying as your previous work. This can easily prolong your depression, because you haven't fully replaced what was lost. Before you can begin to form an attachment to your new job, you have to release your old position and become nonattached to it.

For many, this is extremely difficult. Even when they begin to feel better about the new job, whenever some disappointment occurs, they revert to their previous state of dissatisfaction and begin to reconstruct their original loss all over again. This vacillation between feeling good and feeling bad can be debilitating and stressful.

To complete the grieving process, therefore, you have to achieve this state of nonattachment. In my experience, that only comes about when you sincerely seek God's grace and ask for the power to help you release what was taken from you. Our natural instinct is to hold on to everything. Only God can gradually remove your fingers so that the object or person falls free from your grasp and you can get on with your life without it.

The portion of Scripture I've found most helpful in working with Christian patients is Philippians 3:7-12. In fact, the whole of Philippians 3 is extremely helpful in this regard. The central point of what Paul says is contained in verse 7: "But what things were gain to me, those I counted loss for Christ" (KJV).

The phrase "I counted loss" describes a decision on Paul's part. It was his intentional choice that everything he had counted gain, including being considered a righteous Jew who had zealously persecuted the church, was no longer important to him. And the reason he could count those things as loss was that he had found something far better. The "excellency of the knowledge of Christ Jesus my Lord" (v. 8) made the difference.

Paul had adjusted his values so that the only thing that mattered in life was God and His message to the world through Christ. With such a value system, it's no wonder he could rejoice even in the closing moments of his life, when he was about to lose everything.

To become a mature Christian, you have to be able to separate the *essentials* of life from the *nonessentials*. Think about your life and its many facets, and then ask yourself: Is this an essential facet or a nonessential? If you have God's perspective, only things of eternity will fall into the category of "essential." All other matters become nonessential.

Pray that God will constantly remind you of whether something is an essential

tendency to idealize

or a nonessential issue of life. If you can do that, depression will certainly become less of a problem for you. You will be able to move quickly to the place of acceptance and nonattachment.

What can I learn about depression from people in the Bible?

The most important lesson is that depression is the common experience of everyone, even great saints of God. No one is exempt. It's a process designed into us by an intelligent God as a healing experience. The study of people like Elijah and King David, whose emotions are vividly described, confirms this.

Second, while we have to live out the gospel in the context of our humanity, a study of biblical characters helps us come to terms with our limitations and discover how God can enable us to transcend them.

We have a strong tendency to idealize not only characters from the Bible, but also ministers. We need to realize that their acts of faith are in the context of a very normal humanity. Being reminded of that, we can accept ourselves and turn to God in our depression rather than turning to a state of despair.

Nothing causes more despair than the deep-seated fear that you're never going to make it or that everyone else is more spiritual than you. But that's not what the gospel is all about. Look at those Old Testament characters. See how human they were. Reflect on how exactly like you they were. But then see what they were able to do for God, and take courage from their victories.

How can I keep up my spiritual life when I feel so low?

Never give in to the temptation to abandon your spiritual life when you're depressed: "Let me just set aside my walk with God and deal with my problems first. Then I'll get back to it." No, your spiritual life must be brought into harmony with the whole experience of depression. If you do that, you will find your spiritual life helps and complements the other.

To keep your spiritual life vital when you feel down, you must accept the depression. I don't mean you resign yourself to it, but you should accept your emotion for what it is—a symptom that something is wrong and needs attention.

You don't have to be preoccupied with it. A lot of depression can just be "set aside." You know it's there, but you don't have to dwell on it. Many people learn to disregard pain and live with it. In a sense, you need to disregard your depression in the same way. You also need to avoid allowing the *feeling* of depression to keep you from dealing with the *cause* of it. The resources of Christ will enable you to do that.

WHEN I'M DEPRESSED, I DON'T WANT TO READ MY BIBLE AND PRAY. IS THERE ANY HOPE FOR ME?

There's a lot more to spiritual devotion than just reading your Bible or praying. Even though your depression robs you of the energy of concentration to focus on some specific Bible study or a purposeful act of praying, there's still a lot you can do. Remember, God understands how you feel better than you do.

For example, you can meditate on God or Scripture just where you sit or lie. Quietly open yourself up to receive from Him whatever He wants to give you. Rather than trying to concentrate on giving out to Him in some specific devotional activity, relax and receive from Him. Meditation should be the natural consequence of being depressed. It doesn't take energy, you can do it when you're down, and it can be more meaningful than concentrated reading or even prayer at such times.

DOES DEPRESSION ARISING FROM SIN REQUIRE DIFFERENT TREATMENT FROM THAT ARISING FROM LOSS?

In some ways, yes. A depression arising from sinful behavior has to be treated by first dealing with the sin. While the sin continues to exist, there will be no relief from the depression. We deal with sin, of course, by repentance and confession, as set out in 1 John 1:9.

Many losses also arise secondary to the sin: loss of self-respect, of the peace of God, of His closeness, and so on. But the treatment must first involve recognition of the sin, confession of the sin, repentance, and the acceptance of forgiveness—the whole package. Even when you've gone through these steps and have received by faith the forgiveness of God through Christ, however, you may still find yourself feeling depressed. There are losses still to be grieved, and you must avoid becoming depressed over the fact that you still feel depressed.

IS PRAYER A PSYCHOTHERAPEUTIC PROCESS?

Prayer is much more than therapy. It's true that it produces growth and self-understanding, but we can't reduce prayer just to the therapeutic. Therapy is a process requiring another person, but that other person can be God just as well as another human being. God doesn't expect us to communicate only with Him, however. We need one another, and sharing with other human beings is also in God's plan for our wholeness. A great deal of emphasis ought to be put on the fellowship of believers, the dependence we have on one another in the body of Christ for emotional healing. Fellowship with God in prayer and fellowship with others in the body are both essential.

CAN I PRAY MY WAY OUT OF A DEPRESSION?

It depends on the depression, or more importantly on what's causing it. If it's caused by sin, yes, you can pray your way out of it. The act of prayer involves confession, repentance, and the receiving of forgiveness, so you remove the cause of the depression. You can get up from that kind of praying and really believe you've received forgiveness. Keep in mind what I've just mentioned, though, that the *feeling* of depression may not go away immediately.

Praying also helps to put things into perspective. It gets you in touch with the resources of God, too. But I don't want to give the impression that every time you're depressed, you can just pray and it will go away. It's not that easy. But prayer needs to be an integral part of your healing from depression.

CAN I PRAISE MY WAY OUT OF A DEPRESSION?

Some preachers have suggested you can praise yourself out of a depression. It's not that easy. If you're over the worst part of your depression, you can speed your recovery with acts of praise. But while you're heavy with the loss, it's difficult to praise. In fact, trying to praise at that point can intensify the depression. God wants us to have an attitude of praise, but an act of praising must come from an appropriate feeling.

Once you have come through the worst of the depression and are beginning to feel it lift, praising can speed up the recovery. One important aspect of praise is that it focuses your attention on positive things. You count your blessings. That in turn helps you to regain perspective on your losses. So praise at this stage can certainly help you to get over the final stage of your depression more quickly.

HOW CAN I THANK GOD FOR WHAT SEEMS TO BE A SENSELESS AND HOPELESS SITUATION?

Thanking God in a hopeless situation can only be meaningful if you really understand how things fit together in His kingdom. If you have His perspective on this life, you can thank God even though your circumstances seem hopeless, useless, and pointless.

Colossians 3:15-16 tells us we should "let the peace of Christ rule in your hearts. . . . And be thankful. Let the word of Christ dwell in you richly." When God's Word dwells in you, you have a deeper understanding of the larger scheme of things. You know God's plan. You begin to see the essential nature of the eternal compared to the nonessential nature of temporal things. All of this put together gives you a perspective from which you can thank God even in the middle of the deepest depression, for behind that deep, low mood, you have the conviction that there's a plan and a purpose in it all, and you can thank God for it.

S I X

Coping with Depression

Part 2

endogenous

Perhaps you wonder if you can simply "grow out" of having depression. It depends on the type of depression. Many endogenous depressions stop spontaneously. Others get better when you reduce the stress in your life. You can grow out of reactive depressions by maturing out of them. One of the advantages of growing older is that you develop a measure of maturity from the experiences life gives you. You learn that some losses are temporary and that other losses, while permanent, are not that important.

You don't grow out of depression in the sense that you'll be free of all depression. If anything, you'll be more prone to depression as you get older. Your physiology is aging, and your systems are less resilient. Added to those physical losses, there are economic and social losses as well. But there's the counterbalance of maturity. If you learn to master life, then the older you get, the more of a master you become. That's why you need to maximize your sanctification (your spiritual growth and development) early in life. The better you adjust to an early stage, the better you'll be able to adjust to later stages.

That's not to say you can't reduce a lot of unnecessary depression, however. Much of what I've talked about so far is designed to reduce the frequency of depression. Probably half the depressions most of us experience can be avoided if we really work at changing our value systems and allow ourselves to grieve in a healthy way. God helps us to heal our selfishness and self-preoccupation through our depressions.

WILL A CHANGE OF CIRCUMSTANCES HELP ME OUT OF A DEPRESSION?

If your circumstances are causing you many losses or too much stress, a change will help. Taking a vacation or a trip may enable you to see things differently. Changing your circumstances may also give you a chance to rest and relax by taking you out of your regular routine. Busy people, especially, need a change frequently.

IF MY DEPRESSION IS TRIGGERED BY CIRCUMSTANCES THAT SEEM UNLIKELY TO CHANGE, HOW CAN I HOPE TO AVOID A RECURRING DEPRESSION?

This is the case for the many people who face losses that can't be replaced. Bereavement, including the grief that follows, is a good example. In losing a loved one, perhaps a husband who was the sole source of income, you face an irreversible situation. Besides grieving the loss through your depression, you must also begin to adjust to the permanent nature of the loss and to take control of your circumstances. It may require several major changes in your life.

To use another analogy, if you're running an obstacle race and come up against an insurmountable obstacle, you have to find a way around it. It's exactly the same way when you encounter circumstances beyond your control. You have to learn to compensate for what you cannot change in order to find a way around. For some, this may involve drastic changes, such as selling a home or reducing your standard of living. But you must take control and find a way around your obstacles.

I must also emphasize again that when circumstances seem to be beyond your control, the tendency is to revert to a state of helplessness. That only intensifies the depression. A loss of control, which is part of the helplessness, can cause the most intense form of depression. So it's vital that you take control of your circumstances and begin to design your life around a new set of "givens." If you fail to do that, your depression will not lift.

THE CAUSE OF MY DEPRESSION HAS DISAPPEARED, BUT I STILL FEEL DEPRESSED. WHAT'S THE MATTER WITH ME?

That brings up an important point that needs to be driven home. Depression is not just in your head. It's not just a psychological experience. It may be triggered psychologically, but it affects the whole body. A fairly massive biochemical shift takes place when you become depressed. Glands, muscles, and many other parts respond with changes. In fact, the low, sad mood and the lethargy you feel are all a result of those biochemical changes. Primarily the depression is designed to slow you down and remove you from your environment.

When the cause of the depression is removed or resolved, the feeling does not immediately go away. It may hang on for many hours, even days, depending on how long you've been depressed. Your biological system needs time to restore itself. The disturbed chemistry has to "burn" itself out and pass from your system. Only then will the feeling of depression disappear. It's important, therefore, not to become impatient and react to the lingering feeling. That will only chain other emotions and prolong the depression.

IF IT'S IMPORTANT TO MAINTAIN SOME LEVEL OF INTROSPECTION, HOW DO I ACHIEVE A BALANCE BETWEEN TOO MUCH AND TOO LITTLE?

You need to maintain a balance between avoiding all introspection (which is quite common) and becoming preoccupied with what goes on inside. The balance is not in the amount of inward looking you do but in *what* you do with what you find there. Clearly, we all sometimes need to do some looking deep within ourselves.

The unhealthy aspect of introspection comes when you're so preoccupied with yourself that you become self-rejecting. That leads to depression. It causes you to punish yourself and become despondent.

A healthy introspection involves looking at yourself objectively, analyzing what you're doing, and using that information as a map or plan to guide your self-improvement. You say, "Well, this part of my nature is not very good. I tend to get angry easily. And every time I get angry, I become depressed. If I want to deal with this depression, I've got to learn to become less angry."

Continuing the process, you analyze why you become angry. You learn you're very prone to frustration; you want everything to happen right away. By recognizing this tendency, you can begin to deal with it, to reduce your anger, and thus avoid some depression. This results in self-growth and self-development.

Can someone else help in this process?

An outside point of reference can be very helpful. You can't always trust yourself. You need a sounding board. The other person doesn't need to be a psychological expert, either, just someone who knows how to listen. You bounce your findings off the person, who either confirms or helps you to correct what you're feeling about yourself.

How can I change a negative thinking spiral?

A negative thinking spiral is a tendency to feed your mind with negative thoughts in such a way as to keep the depression going. The negative thoughts become self-perpetuating.

I am primarily a "cognitive" psychologist. That means I lay a lot of stress on what's going on in the head. Your thinking is the key to controlling your emotions and behavior. While thinking doesn't cause all feelings, it's at least the starting point for correcting your troubled feelings.

Proverbs 23:7 tells us that "as [a man] thinketh in his heart, so is he"(KJV). There's a lot of practical truth in that idea. The gospel comes to us with a rational and logical system of values and beliefs. That system runs counter to the erroneous ideas, misbeliefs, and illogical thinking patterns of our world, which feed the negative thinking spiral.

To correct your thinking, then, you should allow the truths of the gospel to saturate your mind. That's not easy to do by yourself, so again it's wise to find someone else to help you evaluate your thinking and encourage you to make changes. A small group of supportive friends can do this for each other. We need to be in an open relationship with others to be healthy. (I'll be talking more about this in chapter 7.)

Will acting as if I feel good help me to really feel good?

Sometimes, but not always. It depends on where you are in your depression. When you've "bottomed out," you're through the deepest part, and your grieving is done. You can now speed up the recovery phase by just behaving as if you feel good again. That helps to build your confidence and reinforces your improvement. Get back into your normal routine. Put a smile on your face. That breaks the tendency to be self-pitying. Very soon you will find that you begin to feel good again.

I repeat, however, that this is only helpful during the recovery phase. In the earlier phases, such behavior will usually just aggravate the depression. Your body or mind is not ready to give up the depression.

ONE OF THE MOST DIFFICULT PROBLEMS IN DEPRESSION IS THE RELATIONSHIP BETWEEN THE WILL AND FEELINGS. HOW CAN I GET MY WILL MOTIVATED WHEN I FEEL SO DOWN?

The secret is to learn to "disregard" or "step over" your feelings. Now, that doesn't mean you ignore or deny them. Feelings are important symptoms and must be attended to. But once you've recognized you have certain feelings, you can choose whether or not to continue dwelling on them. (We'll be discussing this more thoroughly in chapter 7.)

HOW CAN I DO WHAT I KNOW I SHOULD WHEN I DON'T FEEL LIKE DOING ANYTHING AT ALL?

If you know what you should do and you don't feel like doing it, you have a choice. You can just not do it, or you can exercise some willpower and go ahead and do it anyway. Depression diminishes willpower, but it doesn't take it away. If you *believe* you can do something, even though you don't feel like doing it, you can do it. It comes right back again to the nature of your beliefs.

Take the mother who is experiencing a depression following the birth of her child. She knows the child must be fed, but she doesn't feel like doing it. Yet she goes ahead and feeds the child because she knows it must be done.

Why should that be any different from other circumstances where a person knows what must be done but doesn't feel like doing it? The difference is simply that in the one case there is a strong conviction that the act must be done. In other words, the person doesn't really believe it's that important. What you have to do, then, is to strengthen your belief about what must be done.

WHAT'S A GOOD WAY TO START THE DAY WHEN I DON'T EVEN FEEL LIKE GETTING OUT OF BED?

Always start the day by committing it to God. Do this before you even try to get out of bed. Then you must resort to sheer willpower. A spouse or friend can also be helpful in encouraging you to just start getting up. Take it one step at a time. Slowly you will accomplish what seems to be an overwhelming task.

IS TAKING SOME POSITIVE ACTION HELPFUL IN COMBATING DEPRESSION?

Most definitely. Taking positive action, no matter how small, helps to maintain a sense of control. You have to avoid feeling helpless at all costs. Retreating and just letting things happen to you accentuates and feeds the depression. Even so small a positive action as tying your shoelaces can build some feeling of control.

Let me give you a concrete example of beginning to take positive action. Suppose you have lost your job, and you feel a deep depression coming on. The first step may be just to sit down with a piece of paper and write out a résumé. Perhaps looking in the newspaper for job openings can be the first step. Another step might be to get some vocational guidance counseling, to see if you're in the right line of work.

IS THIS TRUE ON BOTH THE DOWNWARD SIDE AND THE RECOVERY SIDE OF DEPRESSION?

Yes, positive action is helpful wherever you are in your depression. It's perhaps more effective on the recovery side, but "taking control" is a step you can begin at any point. If you don't, it's easy to get deeper and deeper into a depression. You create a sense of helplessness that puts you at the mercy of your circumstances. Often the sense of lost control creates a much greater loss than the original one.

DON'T ASSERTIVE PEOPLE FIND THEMSELVES FRUSTRATED BY CIRCUMSTANCES OVER WHICH THEY HAVE NO CONTROL?

Surprisingly, individuals who are able to take control of their personal circumstances usually have a better understanding of their limitations and are much more accepting of conditions they can't master. People who have difficulty asserting their rights often feel helpless in all areas of life.

When the apostle Paul said "I have learned to be content whatever the circumstances" (Phil. 4:11), I think he was saying much the same thing. He understood his own limitations, yet when called upon to exercise authority, he was able to do so.

HOW IS IT POSSIBLE TO TAKE CONTROL OVER GLOBAL CIRCUMSTANCES?

I'm talking here mainly about ordinary circumstances in life—your job, family, church—over which you *can* take control. Some circumstances are truly beyond your control, such as the weather, the national economy, and even world affairs. There must be a certain resignation to such circumstances in order to maintain a healthy attitude. If our country decides to go to war, it's going to happen whether you like it or not. In such circumstances, it would be impossible for you to "take control."

Unfortunately, many people become too taken up with the kinds of circumstances just mentioned and so suffer more depression than is necessary. We can't allow global events to make us feel so helpless that we're constantly depressed. We have to accept that there is much we can't control and leave it be.

SOMEONE HAS SAID, "A PURCHASE A DAY KEEPS DEPRESSION AWAY." IS SPENDING MONEY A GOOD WAY TO COUNTER DEPRESSION?

It's true that when some people are depressed, they counter it by spending money. They indulge themselves in such a way that, temporarily, the depression doesn't seem so bad. The more money they spend, the more it relieves their depression. Mind you, it can be a costly way to cope with depression. If you spend too much, you have another loss to deal with afterward.

Some people resort to spending because they're reinforcement-deprived. They either don't have many positive things going on in their lives, or they're not being positively reinforced for the things they're doing. Many housewives find themselves in such a predicament. Life can be dull when all you do is wash clothes, cook meals, and discipline kids. These women are caught up in their housework and are not adequately reinforced in their life's experiences. So they may go on an occasional spending spree to make themselves feel better and to provide the missing reinforcement.

If you're reinforcement-deprived, work at building some reinforcing experiences into your everyday life-style. Solid friendships, occasional outings, or a change in your routine can provide satisfying elements. That way you won't have to depend on spending money for your good feelings. Some spouses need to be more attentive here and help to provide more variety for the homebound spouse's life.

IF I'M ALREADY DEPRESSED BECAUSE OF FINANCIAL PROBLEMS, WON'T SPENDING MONEY ON A PROFESSIONAL COUNSELOR WORSEN THE SITUATION?

Not necessarily. Seeing a counselor may help to speed your recovery. Counseling doesn't have to be expensive, either. Many medical insurance policies include payment for these services, for psychologists as well as psychiatrists. Every city has mental health facilities that charge a minimum fee, usually on a sliding scale tied to income. Further, many churches offer counseling by trained lay people that can provide effective help for milder depressions. If a depression is serious, I don't think you have any option but to obtain competent professional help. The consequences of not getting it can be serious.

HOW CAN I COPE WITH DEPRESSION WHEN I'VE LOST ALL HOPE AND FEEL LIKE ENDING IT ALL?

If you get to the point where your hope is so low that you're thinking about taking your life or running away, you should seek outside help immediately. You can't trust your perceptions when you're in a deep depression. You must have someone else to help you, someone you can share your problems with and who can provide support.

SHOULD I SEEK OUT A FRIEND WHO HAS ALSO EXPERIENCED DEPRESSION OR AN EXTROVERTED, OUTGOING FRIEND?

What you should look for, above all else, is a friend who is understanding and willing to listen without judging you. Whether the person has experienced depression is unimportant. In fact, some people who have been depressed are not easy to speak to because they want to talk about their own depression rather than listen to yours. An extroverted friend may want to short-circuit the process and cut you off. That won't be helpful, either. To repeat, what you need is a friend who has the ability to listen, not give advice.

HOW SHOULD I GO ABOUT DISCUSSING MY DEPRESSION WITH A FRIEND?

At the very beginning, you should make an informal agreement, "structuring" the relationship. Don't just drag someone into a corner and say, "I want you to know what's happened this last week," and then dump it on him or her. Friends tend to run away from that approach. You need to ask permission to be candid. You could say, "I've been getting depressed recently, and I don't know why. I need someone to talk to about it. Would you be available? I'd be happy to do the same for you."

In this informal contract, you should spell out your expectations of your friend. Make clear that all you want him or her to do is to listen so that you can come to some understanding of your problem. You can also assure your friend that if he or she has some insight to offer, you would be happy to receive it. Preparing a friend in this way can be very helpful in making sure the process works properly.

Won't my friends misunderstand and think I'm only asking for pity?

That's all the more reason you should explain beforehand what you expect of your friends. Be straightforward. "I don't want pity from you, and I don't want advice necessarily. All I need is for you to listen." That should avoid any misunderstanding.

Many churches offer lay counseling programs that train their members to be effective listeners. This training also helps counselors to avoid feeling guilty because they can't change a situation dramatically in a short time. Such programs not only train good lay counselors, but they also produce better friends.

What other steps should I take in using my friend effectively?

I would add that in structuring the relationship, you should clarify the time commitment. Don't expect your friend to be available every day for as long as you want. Set some limits, and don't abuse the privilege. It's helpful to ask your friend to give, say, an hour a week for a certain number of weeks. Be frank and honest in setting limits. That will help your friend avoid feeling guilty when the time is up; it's what you agreed to.

When you talk with your friend, explore your loss, lay it out clearly, and talk about the various aspects of it. Often just describing it and exploring its many aspects helps to put it in perspective. You may discover that the way you're thinking or feeling doesn't make sense. Your friend can then help straighten out your thinking.

Am I in danger of depressing others by relating my experiences?

Generally speaking, if you have contracted well, explained your expectations, and set limits on your friendship, you can share your depression without fearing you'll depress your friend also. Depression itself is not contagious. There are some people, though, who are very sensitive and too sympathetic rather than empathetic. They're likely to let your feelings affect them. That doesn't help you, either, because you need understanding rather than sympathy. If you have such a friend, it's better that you don't discuss your feelings with him or her.

How do I respond to friends who say, "Come on, snap out of it. This has gone on long enough"?

Friends who say that are being callous and doing a great injustice. If you could snap out of your depression, you would. Basically, what they're saying is, "Hey, your depression makes me feel depressed, and I would appreciate it if you would stop being depressed so I can feel more comfortable." You can either ask them to stop short-circuiting your depression or seek out other friends.

What can I say to people who insist that all depressions, including mine, are spiritual?

The tendency on the part of some Christians to spiritualize all depressions is dangerous. This is a common theme in the teaching of many popular preachers, and it has been around a long time.

Job heard that thought when God tested him with affliction. His friends tried to comfort him by asking, "Is not your wickedness great? Are not your sins endless?" (Job 22:5). Job had already responded, "Miserable comforters are you all!" (Job 16:2), and he was right! He knew he hadn't sinned, and in the end God vindicated him. But in between, he did suffer from depression. And this is true for all of us—depression is not necessarily tied to sin.

Spiritualizing depression is too simplistic and is certainly not scriptural. Many people sin but never get depressed. Unfortunately, many Christians who have not necessarily sinned get depressed. The best we can say is that *sometimes* there is a connection between sin and depression, but it's not always there.

Another common mistake is to think of depression as being caused or perpetuated by lack of faith in God. This implies that if you were deeply spiritual, you would not get depressed or would get over your depression quickly. If you don't, you're a spiritual failure.

That idea tends to make a person more depressed. Such a person is feeling bad enough as it is. Pile more guilt on top of the depression and you can almost guarantee the individual will be depressed for a long time. Satan must surely clap his hands with glee when we do this.

Another common idea is that healing from depression is exclusively a spiritual exercise. Some preach and teach that *all* depression is healed by simply confessing it, repenting of it, and turning back to God.

This idea fails to recognize that many of our depressions have roots in biochemical or genetic causes, or that a legitimate spiritual discipline needs to be exercised through our depressions. I am a strong believer that God can help us in the healing process and that when it's an entirely spiritual matter, He provides the healing. But in many instances, our depression needs help in addition to whatever prayer or confession we need to make.

We readily acknowledge that when we come across someone whose leg has been crushed in an accident, we should quickly call for paramedics and pray that God will work through surgeons to bring healing. Well, the many depressions that have physical causes are no different from broken bones or an inflamed appendix. Unfortunately, we can't see the broken nerves or the biochemical disturbances that are causing the depression.

As Christians, we need to be open to God's miraculous interventions. There are times when He provides healing without any physical interference or psychological assistance. Many people, however, need to be pointed to the resources of the gospel and to see what they are doing in their personal lives that can be causing or perpetuating their depression.

The Christian counselor has a role, therefore, in facilitating the healing process. God's Spirit is as much present in the counseling room as He is in the pew. God's word speaks through the wisdom of Christian psychologists and helpers as much as it does through the voice of preachers.

We need a holistic healing approach. We need God's help, but we also need to be willing to open our hearts to God before He can heal them. Christian counselors have spiritual resources that can help you to open your heart and be receptive to His healing work.

If you are totally isolated and don't have access to a friend, counselor, or pastor for whatever reason, however, I want to assure you that God understands your condition and will make adequate provision for your healing. Turn now and surrender your life to Him. Pray for His healing, and then claim it by faith.

IS THERE VALUE IN ATTENDING SELF-HELP GROUPS FOR DEPRESSED PEOPLE?

Self-help groups are primarily support groups. They can be extremely helpful for many personal problems. I prefer them to be Christian, however, because some groups can be damaging to your faith if they're not. Often they're designed to break down your beliefs, and if your faith is different from that of other members of the group, they will attack and seek to destroy your faith.

Christian self-help groups should build your faith. They can provide you with resources to help you understand yourself and the causes of your depression. They also provide accountability for you as you contract with them to change some things in your life to help you in your depression. Finally, they can aid you through the most difficult times of your depression. If there is no such group in your church, you may want to consider starting one yourself.

SHOULD THESE GROUPS NECESSARILY BE GROUPS OF DEPRESSED PEOPLE?

No. In fact, I would generally avoid putting a lot of depressed people together in one group. Each depressed person wants to focus on his or her own depression. Such a group would have little to give to each other. *Recovered* depressed people may be helpful in a support group; they can offer perspective on the whole process and provide encouragement to the depressed by describing their own journey. But a "mixed" group works better.

WHERE CAN I GET MATERIAL TO HELP ME UNDERSTAND MY DEPRESSION?

The first and most important resource is your Christian bookstore. Many books written from a Christian perspective are available today. Be careful, however. Some writers really don't understand depression and present it as an alien experience. Avoid such books.

HAVE YOU FOUND ANY BOOKS THAT ARE PARTICULARLY HELPFUL IN THIS AREA?

One that has been helpful to a number of my clients is *Happiness Is a Choice* (Baker Book House), written by two medical doctors, Frank Minirth and Paul Meier. My own books *Unlocking the Mystery of Your Emotions* and *Counseling the Depressed*, both published by Word, should also prove helpful.

WHAT ARE SOME THINGS I CAN DO TO AVOID DEPRESSION IN THE FUTURE?

The best way to prevent future depressions is to deal effectively with your present one. But there are also some prevention measures you can take. One key is to *exercise*.

Time and again, it has been demonstrated that a good exercise program helps seriously depressed people not only to recover more quickly from their depression, but also to prevent future depressions. Exercise can't do this by itself; other aspects of the depression must be treated as well. But since depression tends to create a state of lethargy, stimulating the physical systems by exercise is extremely helpful. It counters the natural tendency to give in to the heaviness that only intensifies the depression.

A balanced *diet* is also important. I encourage my clients to take a vitamin B complex to supplement their normal diet, since most modern foods are deficient there. That helps to prevent some fatigue problems that may develop.

Developing *good relationships* with others is also a preventative. If you have trouble relating to people, I suggest you seek counseling.

It's important that you have a *fulfilling life*. If your job is not fulfilling, for example, you may have to decide if a change would be beneficial.

Underlying all this, of course, should be a *healing faith*, a sound theology, regular Bible reading, prayer, and involvement in Christian activities. The development of a biblical value system is vital in preventing depression.

ARE THERE PARTICULAR EXERCISES THAT ARE BENEFICIAL?

The amount and kind of exercise you should do depends on your physical condition. Your medical doctor is the best person to advise you on how much and what type of exercise you can take. A number of good exercise books start you out with a little bit of exercise and gradually work you up to more-vigorous levels. Many health clubs and YMCAs also have well-designed programs for physical fitness.

Exercises I advocate include riding a bicycle, doing some light jogging, and push-ups and sit-ups if you're physically able. Walking is always healthy, so do as much as you possibly can. Taking a brisk walk with your spouse, children, or dog just before you retire for bed is an excellent practice.

HOW DOES BLOOD-SUGAR LEVEL RELATE TO DEPRESSION?

Sugars exaggerate the normal cycle of highs and lows in the emotions of some people. If you have a tendency to trigger a depression from sugar, see your doctor for a glucose-tolerance test, as you may be prediabetic. It's a fairly standard test to determine whether a person's insulin system is in proper balance for handling large doses of sugar. In general, we should all cut back on sugars as much as we can. We should also avoid extreme amounts of coffee and cola drinks because of the caffeine, which is quite a powerful drug. Moderation is the best policy.

YOU'VE MENTIONED THAT EVEN A REACTIVE DEPRESSION INVOLVES THE BODY'S BIOCHEMICAL SYSTEM. CAN A PROPER DIET SPEED RECOVERY FROM SUCH A DEPRESSION?

Someone who is not in good physical health or who is not eating a balanced diet will not tolerate a reactive depression as well as someone who is fit. In other words, although the trigger for such a depression is psychological (a loss), the way your body reacts will be determined to some extent by your physical condition. A healthy body helps us to have a healthy mind. If your body is in poor shape, relatively minor losses can trigger massive depressions. But if your system is in good health, the physiological components of the depression will not be as intense, and certainly not as prolonged.

IN THE CASE OF THE PHYSICALLY UNFIT, WILL THE BODY'S BIOCHEMISTRY DRAG THEM DOWN FURTHER INTO DEPRESSION?

Yes, an unfit body also means the body's biochemistry is not well balanced. The depression makes you lethargic, and you put out less physical energy; that in turn contributes to further depression. The less healthy your physiology, the more likely the depression will intensify.

S E V E N

Self-Management of Depression

Exogenous depression is one of those emotional experiences that lends itself well to self-management. In this chapter, I want to expand on some of the principles I have already touched on and provide a more systematic description of self-management strategies. They can be applied effectively to yourself, by parent to child, by friend to friend, or by spouse to spouse.

I must stress, however, that if your depression does not respond to a short period of self-management, you should consult a professional, especially to rule out significant biological factors or to get more-sophisticated help. Most depression sufferers, however, can help their healing by some self-management.

WHAT ARE THESE SELF-MANAGEMENT STRATEGIES YOU'RE TALKING ABOUT?

I will present the strategies in the form of seven steps. In summary they are:

1. Planning your strategy for coping
2. Catching negative thoughts
3. Answering negative thoughts
4. Targeting problems you need to change
5. Identifying and changing underlying beliefs
6. "Stepping over" your feelings
7. Learning to really relax

ARE THESE STRATEGIES CONSISTENT
WITH OUR CHRISTIAN BELIEFS?

Most definitely so. Again and again, Scripture reminds us that we're responsible for what we think and for controlling the activities of our minds. God has promised to help us to renew our minds and calls upon us not to be conformed to the pattern of this world (see Rom. 12:2).

Right at the outset, therefore, make sure God is a part of your plan. Ask Him to guide you and give you the wisdom and courage to make the changes needed to bring your depression under control. Turn the exercise into a spiritual one in which your goal is not only to understand yourself better, but also to understand God better and how He works in your life.

WHAT DO YOU MEAN BY PLANNING
YOUR STRATEGY FOR COPING?

Since the major problem with depression is that it slows you down and disturbs your normal activities, you need to plan a strategy for getting through each day and accomplishing tasks that must be fulfilled. The following steps can be helpful:

Make a list of the things you need to do today. Don't try to overplan, but focus on the essential things. You can include work tasks or, if you're a housewife, jobs that must be accomplished at home. Try to focus on three or four major tasks. List them in their order of importance. If your work is assigned by a supervisor, what you have to plan is not so much the tasks to be performed but the attitudes you need to help you complete your assignments.

Try to break each task down into clear steps. For instance, if you want to clean the windows of your home, write down the individual steps that must be taken in the order in which they must be performed. For instance, you might say:

Get bucket and fill it with water.
Add cleaner to water.
Start with kitchen windows.
Then follow with living room and bedroom windows.

Spelling out the individual steps is crucial. When you're depressed, you can't think clearly. You feel overwhelmed by global tasks but can handle "little steps" better. Alternatively, if you're a salesperson, you may want to break down the task of calling on clients into these specific steps:

Prepare list of five clients to call or visit.
Get addresses or telephone numbers of each, etc.

Writing down the steps in this detail might seem like overkill, but be assured that when you're depressed, it's difficult to keep those simple tasks in your head. Unless you've written them out clearly ahead of time as a series of steps, you can feel immobilized. You can also get a friend or spouse to help you break down the steps.

Once you have them clearly outlined, all you have to do is to follow the steps as best you can. This will help you not to feel so overwhelmed by the enormity of the task. Concentrate on completing each step and you'll find you can get through the day more effectively.

Keep a careful record of each task you accomplish so as to reinforce your progress. When you're depressed, it's hard to get a sense of completion or to have any understanding of how much progress you're making. By keeping a careful record of each step taken and each task accomplished, you'll be able to go back, see your progress, and reinforce it in your own mind.

Try to take these tasks one day at a time. In other words, don't try to plan tomorrow's tasks until you have finished those for today. If you don't finish one day's tasks, carry them over to the next day. Set a time each evening or early the next morning to plan your work.

HOW CAN I STOP MY NEGATIVE THINKING?

One of the more debilitating consequences of depression is that it causes many negative thoughts. Those thoughts feed the depression and often perpetuate it unnecessarily. It's important that you try to catch your negative thoughts *as they occur* so you can challenge and reverse them. This helps to stop feeding losses into your mind.

The most effective way to do this is to prepare, either on a sheet of paper or in a notebook, a "thought register." Draw two columns, a narrow one on the left where you can record the date and time, and a wide one on the right where you can write the particular negative thought you're having.

Sometimes it's difficult to recognize when you're having a negative thought. So set a watch or an alarm to signal you every half hour or hour. When you hear the alarm, stop and reflect on what you're thinking. If it's negative, capture the thought by writing it down. At other times, you may immediately become aware of a negative thought. Again, write it down. The principle here is to capture every negative, unhealthy thought as it occurs and write it down so you can have a record of what you're thinking.

Some thoughts are automatic thoughts that repeat themselves over and again like a broken record. For instance, you might be saying to yourself: *I'm a failure. I haven't done anything with my life. I'm always going to be depressed. It's never going to get any better.*

Each of those negative thoughts reinforces some idea of loss and helps to keep your depression alive. Whenever you feel sad or want to cry, try to capture the thought you're having at that moment, and set it down in writing. Even if the same thought recurs again and again, write it down each time. That helps to quantify your negative thoughts.

Slowly, as you do this, you will begin to notice there are certain themes that keep replaying themselves. The themes may focus on feelings of uselessness, hopelessness, or ineffectiveness. If you're depressed because you lost your job, for example, you may find your thoughts constantly going back to ideas of what you could have done differently or trying to discover why you were let go. Those are also negative thoughts. They may take the form of a question: "What did I do wrong?" "What could I have done differently?" "What can I do about it now?" Write these questions down as well, because many of them are negative.

What about your positive thoughts? If you're depressed, you're not likely to be having many of them. But if, in moments of relief, you do have some positive thoughts, writing them down as well will help to reinforce them.

WHAT DO I DO AFTER I'VE CAPTURED MY NEGATIVE THOUGHTS?

Immediately after you have captured a negative thought or when you have a moment to review your thought record, examine your list of negative thoughts more closely. If there's a theme, try to pull together all the thoughts on that theme. For instance, if you're thinking about how useless or worthless you are, try to pull that group together, and then ask yourself the following questions:

What is the evidence to support these thoughts?

Are they really true?

Am I taking the issue out of context?

Am I exaggerating the facts?

Am I imagining the "facts"?

Am I asking myself questions that have no answers?

What are the distortions in my thinking?

Force yourself to examine the truthfulness of your negative statements. Some negative thoughts have a partial truth to them, but most are gross exaggerations or even distortions of the truth.

Having examined your negative thoughts in the light of these questions, try to restate the thoughts in a more positive form. In response to the thought *I got fired because I'm a worthless person*, you might say, "I lost my job because the economic situation is bad." Obviously, if you lost your job because you were dishonest or did not perform your tasks adequately, what you're dealing with is not a negative thought but a legitimate loss that can only be dealt with by appropriate grieving. Few thoughts of a depressed person are really honest, however.

In other words, having captured your negative thoughts, your next goal is to turn them around and rephrase them in a more positive light whenever you can. It's important that you remain honest, but honesty demands that you phrase a negative thought more positively if that thought is not truthful. By continuing to challenge your negative thoughts and turn them into more-positive ones, you will gradually shut off the fire fueling your depression.

Changing thought patterns is a *slow process*. It's like wearing away a stone by dropping water on it. But eventually, turning your negative thoughts into positive ones will begin to have an effect, so be patient in this task. It can help to talk over your negative thoughts with a spouse or close friend to test your perceptions and reformulate your thoughts.

How do I target problems I need to change?

I don't want to give the impression that nothing but thoughts need to be changed in a depressed person's life. It's also important to examine other problem areas needing to be changed.

Here are some key areas you may wish to review and work on:

Procrastination

Inability to enjoy pleasure

Lack of discipline

Lack of mastery of everyday affairs

Avoidance of friends

Excessive self-criticism or self-doubt

Too easily distracted, or problems with concentration

Problems with memory

Difficulty in making decisions

Being overweight or having other physical problems

Too much anxiety and fear

Excessive anger or guilt

Loneliness due to your own social habits

To this list you may want to add several other problems as you think and pray about them. These areas can either cause your depression or be the consequence of it. Try to examine each one and see whether it's the cause or the result of your depression.

Choose one or two of these problem areas as your "target." Let's assume, for instance, that procrastination is a serious problem. You have procrastinated one too many times, and this time you got into serious trouble at work. You kept putting off a certain task that needed to be done, and as a result you were terminated. Now you're deeply depressed, and you lack the energy and drive to look for a new job. The habit of procrastination further prevents you from job hunting. And if you don't deal with this problem promptly, it will likely affect you in your next employment as well. It's a real catch 22!

Having targeted procrastination as a serious hindrance, write down three or four examples of when you procrastinated that got you into trouble. Alongside each of them, try to describe what you could have done differently.

Let's suppose you're a salesman, and you put off making important phone calls. Ask yourself, "What strategies can I devise for dealing with this?" Obviously, you need to start the day by *making a list* of those persons you should call, then placing the calls before you move on to another task. You could ask God for help in keeping your mind focused on the task before you, since the chances are high that you procrastinate because you're easily distracted. The only way to overcome the habit is to force yourself to behave differently.

At the beginning of each day, therefore, write down the tasks that need to be done *before anything else*. Before you move on to some other activity, make sure you have completed those tasks.

It's also possible that the activity you procrastinate on is an unpleasant task for you. We seldom defer pleasurable tasks. A helpful principle is to always precede a pleasant task with an unpleasant one. In other words, *first* do something you don't enjoy, *then* follow with something you do enjoy. You earn the right to do something pleasurable by first doing something unpleasant.

I call this my "grandmother's rule." My grandmother always said to me, "Do the unpleasant thing first, and then you get to do the pleasant thing." Unfortunately, she also applied this rule to food. "First eat your cabbage, and then you get to eat your ice cream." As an adult, I have found this helpful in overcoming my own procrastination. "First make the unpleasant phone call before you make the pleasurable call," I often tell myself. If I make the enjoyable calls first, I find I am out of time before I can make the unpleasant ones.

I've tried to illustrate here how you can deal with procrastination. The same strategy can be applied to the other problem areas you have listed. The strategy is simple:

1. Write down the problem area.

2. Alongside, describe the behaviors that need to be done to reverse the problem.

3. Follow through by giving a high priority to performing those healthier behaviors.

One last thought here: a lack of adequate discipline can be a serious cause of depression in many people. Unfortunately, there is no instant cure for lack of discipline. You need to see it as much as a spiritual problem as it is a psychological one and to ask for spiritual help in dealing with it. In the final analysis, you just have to take control of yourself and do what needs to be done despite your feelings.

How do I identify and change underlying beliefs?

We are all controlled by our beliefs. One of the main features that distinguishes the human mind from that of other life forms is its ability to develop and hold to certain beliefs. This capacity makes it possible for us to have faith and to believe in a God.

But the same system is capable of developing many other beliefs that are not necessarily true and are often "irrational." By *irrational*, I simply mean that beliefs have no basis in reality. They're driven more by emotion than by fact. They are gross distortions of the truth. The human mind has a great affinity for such beliefs, and they're often the cause of unnecessary emotional pain.

For instance, it's irrational to believe that *I am a useless person because every individual I have ever encountered does not value me*. It's an exaggeration, to say the least. There is no reason to expect *every* individual you ever meet to be totally enamored of you. Similarly, it's irrational to believe you should never make a mistake. Making mistakes is inevitable. Of course, it matters whether you're making mistakes 90 percent of the time or only 10 percent of the time, but to be totally free of mistakes is not possible, and to expect it is irrational.

Many unsound beliefs bat around in the heads of otherwise intelligent people. They have a way of eluding recognition simply because they're never challenged. Unfortunately, they also have the ability to cause depression. If, for example, you really believe you should never make a mistake, you'll feel a significant loss when you make one. A series of several mistakes could easily provoke a fairly serious depression.

People who have strong perfectionist tendencies are subject, therefore, to many depressions brought on by the irrational belief that they should be perfect. Since they can't be perfect, they're often confronted by failure.

We all need to survey our beliefs periodically. Make a list of those that seem to be causing you problems now. You may find that some of the thoughts you captured in step two are variations of some irrational belief. For example, a negative thought that says *I will never be normal again because of depression* is clearly based on an irrational conviction. Depressions do not last forever. Even the most severe ones I have worked with ultimately do lift. Only in rare cases does depression continue for a long time.

Write down a negative thought that's bothering you, and then next to it put the irrational belief it's based upon. For example, if you wrote down, "Once you are depressed you can never become undepressed," try to capture the underlying belief. In this case, it might be that "Depression is an incurable disease." Obviously that's not true, so write down a more truthful belief like this: "Sometimes depression is hard to cure, but sooner or later most depressions get better."

You can invariably assume that a negative belief is irrational and should be replaced by a positive one. The belief that "because I have failed on this occasion, I am a total failure" has to be replaced by a more truthful statement: "Just because I failed this time does *not* mean I'm a total failure."

It can be helpful, even for normal and nondepressed people, to examine their irrational beliefs and counter them with more-positive and rational beliefs. If you're severely depressed, you may have great difficulty doing this exercise by yourself, so try to get a friend or spouse to help. Changing your beliefs from irrational to rational may be an extremely slow process, but in due course you will begin to see the benefits.

WHAT DOES IT MEAN TO "STEP OVER MY FEELINGS"?

I don't know why, but it's common for people to believe that because we feel a certain feeling, we must be controlled by it. It's as if some deterministic mechanism has kicked in to control us. Take anxiety, for example. Most people believe that because you feel anxious, you must keep worrying.

This simply isn't true. You don't have to dwell on such feelings, nor do you need to give them any credibility. When you are depressed, your feelings are the result of the depressive process inside you. If you can just understand that these negative feelings have no basis in reality but are symptoms of your depression, you can force yourself to set them aside.

Take guilt, for example. I have a strong tendency to feel guilty even though I've done nothing bad. It goes back to my childhood, when I so often felt responsible for fixing something that had gone wrong in my family.

Now, as an adult, I often feel the same. If one of my daughters asks me to get something for her the next time I'm in town but it would really be inconvenient for me to do it, I might well say no to her request. She accepts my no and understands why I can't do what she wants, yet as I walk away, I begin to feel intensely guilty.

That's called *neurotic guilt*. It's the guilt we feel when there really is no reason for it. By saying no to my daughter, I have not violated any of God's laws. I'm entitled to say no. I am only violating my own arbitrary internal standards of right and wrong. But I still feel guilty.

What do I do with this false guilt feeling? Do I let it control me? Do I allow it to bother me, destroy my peace, or make me depressed? If I don't challenge the feeling, it might well do all of this to me.

Can I remove the feeling? Not always! Even if I challenge my underlying irrational belief, it may still be there. And even when I understand what's causing my neurotic guilt—that it's the consequence of a strict upbringing that made me feel guilty about everything—my feelings remain. So all that's left is for me to ignore the feeling. It's false, and the best I can do is to "step over" it and get on with my life. "Stepping over" is simply my way of saying "disregard the feeling." Do what you believe is the right thing to do, and overlook your emotion.

The "stepping over" image is very useful. We do it in the physical world, and there's no reason we shouldn't also do it emotionally. When we walk along a mountain trail and come across a tree that has fallen in our way, we don't stop and say to ourselves, *There's no way we can go any farther. This tree is blocking us, so we should turn around and go back.* No, we don't accept that from physical obstacles. We climb over the tree trunk and continue our journey on the other side. Many feelings have to be dealt with in exactly the same way.

Let me give another example. When I'm grieving some significant loss in my life, I don't have to allow the sadness to prevent me from moving forward. While I encourage the process of grieving, I might well "step over" the depression, realizing I don't have to be controlled by the feeling. I can say to myself, *I know my sad feeling is part of my depression. I don't have to let that feeling determine what I do. I know what I must do, and I will go and do it.*

Another application is in the realm of anger. Someone may unintentionally do or say something that makes me angry. I realize immediately that the person didn't intend to hurt me, but I feel angry anyway. What am I to do with this feeling? I certainly shouldn't act on it. It would be totally unfair to take my anger out on the person. All that's left for me to do, therefore, is to "step over" my feeling of anger. I can't wait for it to go away. I must disregard it. It's a smoke alarm that goes off without reason. I acknowledge I've heard it, and then I ignore it and get on with the business at hand.

Realizing you don't have to be controlled by your feelings can be very freeing. "Stepping over" can, therefore, be a useful way of dealing with many false and even some real feelings.

How can I learn to really relax?

In my discussion of premenstrual tension (see chapter 3), I outlined a strategy for relaxation. It's possible that if you're a male you didn't read that section. Since my comments here build on the technique I describe there, you may want to review it.

Effective relaxation is an important strategy for dealing with many disorders. Stress symptoms, for example, are greatly reduced when one regularly relaxes. Certain depressions, especially those that are stress related, respond dramatically to regular relaxation exercises. And since depression is itself a stressor that can produce secondary stress symptoms, practicing relaxation when you're depressed can help to relieve your stress symptoms.

The relaxation technique I described in chapter 3 was essentially a form of muscle relaxation. By relaxing all your muscles and remaining immobile, you can produce a fairly profound state of deep relaxation. This is known as the "relaxation response" and is the exact opposite of the "stress response" in which we're mobilized for "fight or flight." When we're deeply relaxed, we can't be under stress. The two responses are totally incompatible. Relaxation displaces stress.

Since the essential mechanism of stress arousal is an increased flow of adrenaline, other techniques can supplement muscle relaxation to produce a more profound state of relaxation.

For example, there's an excellent method of raising the temperature of your hands. No doubt you've noticed that when you're under a lot of stress, your hands get cold. If you've ever had to give a public lecture or preach a sermon, you probably noticed this phenomenon. We all suffer from it, but some of us experience it to a greater extent than others. Some may only cool their hands one or two degrees, whereas others will cool them by as much as ten or 15 degrees. Obviously, you can't cool your hands below the temperature of your environment, but you can come close to it.

What's happening here? During the stress response, your body puts out more adrenaline as its way of mobilizing your system to cope. Your blood pressure goes up, your heart rate increases, and your muscles become more tense. This is the body's way of preparing itself for threat or emergency, and it's why we call it the "fight or flight" response.

To prepare your body for this response, blood has to be redirected to those parts of the body that need it the most. For instance, your heart and brain need more blood for controlling the body, and the stomach and digestive organs need more blood to speed up digestion. That helps the body to perform its tasks more efficiently during the supposed emergency.

This is all good during times of genuine emergency. However, for many of us, stress is often not related to a genuine emergency. It may be caused by something internal or imagined. But the body doesn't know the difference between threats that come from within and those that come from without.

When extra blood is shunted to the heart, brain, muscles, and stomach, it has to come from somewhere—the hands and feet. They don't need much blood to perform their functions during an emergency, so they get colder as they're deprived of blood.

You can test for this cooling effect by putting your hands on your face. If they're colder than your face, you are having a stress response. Your adrenaline is pumping strongly and preparing you for an emergency reaction. If this reaction is prolonged, you'll begin to experience stress symptoms like headaches, ulcers, stomach disturbances, and muscle aches—all related to too much adrenaline.

How can you relax so as to reduce these symptoms? Since the lowering of your hand temperature is one of the effects of adrenaline arousal, in addition to the muscle relaxation technique described in chapter 3, you need to learn how to warm your hands. There are two ways to do that. The first is to relax your *thinking* in such a way that it stops maintaining the state of emergency. The second is to consciously *raise the temperature* of your hands. Together with muscle relaxation, you can then produce a profound state of relaxation.

HOW CAN I RELAX MY MIND?

Relaxing your thinking involves filtering your thoughts and mental activities so as to stop maintaining the state of arousal. You can accomplish this by doing the exercises I have already described. Negative thoughts produce a state of arousal and stress. Positive thoughts do the opposite. By following those exercises, you will "filter" your thoughts and only allow healthy ones to remain, thus producing a lowered state of arousal.

The technique for raising your hand temperature is more physical than mental. Begin by doing the muscle relaxation exercise described in chapter 3. When you feel you're in a fairly deep state of relaxation, turn your concentration to the temperature of your hands. Are they warm or cold? Imagine that you're lying on the beach with the warm sun beating on your arms and hands. Then imagine that the blood vessels in your hands are getting larger and that the body is sending more blood to them. Every now and again, raise your hand and put it against your face to see whether the hand is getting warmer. This is a form of feedback that will help you to know if you're doing the right thing.

Continue this for a while. At first your hands may get colder. This is due to some anxiety over whether you're doing the exercise correctly. Before too long, this will go away. In my book *Adrenalin and Stress*,[1] I describe how you can use temperature dots to help you tell how warm your hands are. These dots can also be used as a form of feedback to confirm whether you're relaxing effectively.

By focusing on hand warming and coupling it with deep muscle relaxation, you can produce a profound state of relaxation. When practiced for as little as 20 or 30 minutes a day, it can help to reduce stress symptoms and speed the healing process even in biologically based depressions. If you have difficulty learning how to relax by yourself, seek help from a psychologist or counselor.

One further word of comment, however. It's common for Christians to think that relaxing their minds and silencing their thoughts gives Satan an opportunity to take control of their minds. I can't think of any idea that is further from the truth. If we're steeped in God and desire His presence above everything else, a state of relaxation such as I have just described can be the perfect opportunity for you to spend time with Him and to allow Him to meet with you in a profound way.

Sadly, many of us are too hurried and busy to ever touch God profoundly. Deep relaxation can provide the ideal opportunity for such a meeting. God can touch us with His healing in new and meaningful ways if we just slow down and spend some quiet and restful time with Him. Be assured that when you empty your mind of the stress and hurriedness that pursues you every day, God will be there to meet with you.

---

1. Archibald D. Hart, *Adrenalin and Stress* (Dallas: Word, 1986, 1988, 1991); 1986, 1988, pp. 121–26; 1991, pp. 101–5.

CAN YOU GIVE SOME KEYS TO MINIMIZING DEPRESSION IN THE FUTURE?

Every depression ought to teach us important lessons about how to minimize the effects in the future. Here are four ways to lessen future depressions:

1. Learn to monitor your thoughts in such a way as to produce a healthier and more positive way of thinking. Besides helping you in your present depression, the exercises I've described, if also carried out during times when you're not depressed, can prevent the onset of your next depression.

2. Learn to recognize the connection between your negative thinking and feelings of depression, and cut off those thoughts earlier. We can't ignore our thinking habits. Many depressed individuals have practiced negative thinking for years. It has become a life-style for them. They have a lot of unlearning to do before they can avoid or minimize future depressions.

3. Think more realistically and honestly, and be more reality based. Fantasy and imagination can feed expectations and lower our tolerance for loss. Ultimately, we all need to realize life is full of losses. The only abiding hope is that which God gives us in Christ. He is our reality.

4. Prevent or minimize future depressions by developing healthier life scripts, or "schemes." A *schema* is a framework of beliefs. The idea "I am a failure" is a schema, because it writes a script for your life. If you believe it, you'll probably behave like a failure. If you hold to such global beliefs, your whole life will be determined by them. Every Christian needs to rewrite his or her life scripts and make sure God is a part of them. We believe God is in control and that Christ is our Savior. This should create a more hopeful outlook so that we can say with Paul, "I have learned the secret of being content in any and every situation" (Phil. 4:11).

HOW CAN THE CHURCH HELP?

There are many ways the church can help those who are depressed beyond providing pastoral or other counseling. This is not to minimize the value of pastoral counseling or even the guidance provided by lay counselors. Those who are depressed need all the help and companionship they can get, but the help the church can give goes way beyond this.

First, I would stress the importance of creating the right attitude in the minds of church members toward those who are depressed. As I've said before, too often, especially in evangelical and more conservative circles, depressed people are shunned, even ostracized, because depression is seen as some form of moral or spiritual failure.

I repeatedly encounter literature from Christian organizations, usually television-based programs, that encourages those in emotional turmoil to call their telephone counseling service. The literature they receive invariably condemns them for being depressed and suggests that God has abandoned them and their depression is due to some moral or spiritual problem. That only makes the depression more painful to bear. The one who is depressed knows well how difficult it is to be spiritually alive, so when he or she feels condemned by other believers, the depression is only intensified.

How can members of a church be sensitized? Clearly, there needs to be some instruction. This can take the form of special Bible studies or special events to which professional persons are invited to teach members how to view and respond to depression. I have conducted many such seminars to great effect.

A sensitive pastor can also educate a congregation through preaching. The Bible has many examples of depressed saints of God, and by building on their experiences, one can teach people how to understand and deal with depression.

Coping with depression should be a fundamental mental health skill we teach to all our church members, who in turn can teach it to their children.

Second, churches can provide healing resources of many sorts. In addition to whatever counseling facility is available through the church, support groups can be set up to help those who are deeply depressed to take care of themselves. Depression distorts spiritual perceptions. It isn't always easy to pray for yourself and to turn toward God in your pain. The help of other believers in Bible study, prayer, and other support activities can go a long way toward sustaining one's faith. Just hearing from others who have also been depressed can greatly facilitate your own recovery.

Third, churches can provide financial support for those among their numbers who are poor and need professional treatment, especially antidepressant medication. If a church is to be Christ's body and a witness to the gospel, it has to take care of emotional needs just as readily as it responds to physical needs. We would certainly rush in to feed a starving member of a congregation, but we often stand by helplessly and watch someone who is impoverished suffer from a depression that could easily be relieved with appropriate treatment.

A special fund could be set up to help people in your neighborhood with emotional needs. It could be a fantastic outreach from a church to a community that could produce a rich harvest of souls. After all, when you're hurting, you're a lot more open to spiritual issues than when you're healthy.

Last, and above all, a church needs to be in much prayer for members' emotional struggles. Times of trouble ought to be times that unite a church, not split it apart. We can't fix everything, nor can we be everywhere at the same time. But prayer is a powerful resource for us. A church that is in much prayer for the emotional needs of its members is a church ready to fulfill Christ's calling to be the bearers of each other's burdens.

E I G H T

Professional Treatment of Depression

Up to this point, much of the material presented has been concerned with so-called self-help: what you can do to help yourself recover from depression. In this chapter, we turn our attention to the professional treatment required by the more serious depressions.

Eighty percent of people with serious depressions can be treated successfully. The sooner the treatment is started, the greater is the likelihood of a successful outcome. Even the most severe forms of depression can respond rapidly to treatment. In fact, it is often the case that the more serious the depression, the more readily it responds to treatment.

Most treatments for depression are conducted in combinations; medication complements counseling or therapy. Such combined methods are often more effective than any one method by itself, but that depends on the nature of the depression. If you suffer from recurring episodes or from mania, you may need to stay on medication all the time in order to prevent or alleviate further occurrences.

WHAT ARE THE MAJOR TYPES OF TREATMENT FOR DEPRESSION?

They can be classified into three groups. The first and most important is psychotherapy or counseling. The difference between them is one of intensity and intent. Psychotherapy is focused on significant personality change, whereas counseling provides guidance and insight in dealing with normal problems. Both use another person with whom we can discuss our feelings and explore what's going on in our lives.

Professionals who work with this treatment include clinical psychologists, psychiatrists, pastoral counselors, and marriage and family counselors. The psychotherapy skills of the clinical psychologist or psychiatrist are focused on the treatment of the more severe forms of depression. They often collaborate to combine psychotherapy with the use of medication.

Psychotherapy is used by itself in the treatment of reactive depressions and combined with other types of treatment in helping the neurotically depressed sufferer.

A second major category of treatment is medication, specifically, the use of antidepressant medication for the treatment of endogenous depressions—those that result from some medical, physiological, or biochemical disturbance. Such treatment is given primarily by a psychiatrist, often in consultation with a clinical psychologist. In recent years, many other medications have also come to be used in endogenous depressions, so this has become a complex field requiring a high degree of specialization.

A third category of treatment, probably the most severe, is the use of electro-convulsive therapy (ECT). It is, unfortunately, grossly misunderstood. It involves giving the brain an electrical impulse that causes a mild seizure while the patient is anesthetized. The procedure is repeated a number of times. ECT is remarkably effective in treating certain severe depressions, especially in the elderly. It is most effective with the endogenous forms of depression.

WHAT IS THE ROLE OF PSYCHOTHERAPY IN TREATING DEPRESSION?

Psychotherapy is a most important technique for treating depression. It's the primary, and often sole, treatment in the reactive or psychological depressions, and it may be used together with the other treatments (medication and ECT) in working on the endogenous depressions.

Psychotherapy is an interaction between people that provides help through someone listening and providing understanding. The process of psychotherapy also helps us to interpret what's going on in our lives and develop insight into what our losses are and how to grieve them.

I would not restrict this therapy to what goes on in the formal, professional sense between a psychologist and a client. Therapy goes on in all healthy relationships. Your spouse and friends can be very helpful in providing understanding. In Christian communities, the whole notion of fellowship—the bearing of one another's burdens and of being there to help, listen, and understand—is what psychotherapy is all about. It just so happens that professional psychotherapists are trained to provide such help more effectively and efficiently.

Is there a relationship between the duration and the intensity of a depression?

Sometimes. Quite often, the more serious endogenous depressions come on rapidly. In a matter of a few days, people can find themselves in a very deep depression. But the deeper the depression, the longer it's likely to last. Reactive depressions, likewise, will be deeper when the loss is greater. Again, the key to when professional help is needed is when things seem to be getting out of control and the depression is interfering with normal duties.

Would you recommend that a Christian choose only a Christian psychotherapist?

Yes, where possible. That doesn't mean a psychotherapist has to be a Christian to be helpful any more than a surgeon has to be a Christian to operate successfully. Nor does it mean that a Christian psychotherapist is necessarily more competent. But psychotherapy does get into some intimate details that often require a client to change or modify values. A secular therapist could, therefore, be hazardous.

As a Christian psychotherapist, I recognize that one of the most important aspects of Christian psychotherapy is the application of God's resources that are available to us. It's important, then, that we see someone who understands the nature of our beliefs and our commitment to the power of God in our lives. Any Christian seeing a non-Christian therapist who frequently challenges or threatens his faith should end the relationship immediately. Christian psychotherapy is now an accepted and available form of treatment.

Are there dangers in a friend or spouse's acting as a psychotherapist?

There are limitations to the help a nonprofessional person can provide. Untrained people should never try to be psychotherapists. For one thing, they don't always understand the finer points of what is going on in the relationship.

They're not trained to understand how certain psychological functions interact or how defenses of various sorts operate. People who have a little knowledge of psychology are perhaps the most dangerous. It's like knowing a little about surgery and so trying to cut and stitch. Once you open up a problem, you may find it far more difficult to contain than you expected.

Another limitation of friends and spouses is the intimacy of the day-to-day relationship with them. Often they can't be as honest or transparent as is needed. Alternatively, they may be too hurtful. Depressed people need help from someone who is not involved in their daily lives, someone who can be impartial. For these reasons, unless the problem is relatively minor, it's often better to go to a professional.

WHAT CAN A PROFESSIONAL COUNSELOR DO FOR US THAT WE CAN'T DO FOR OURSELVES?

A professional counselor provides understanding gained from experience in dealing with depressed persons and from the study of the technical aspects of depression. Also, the professional counselor is trained to provide and communicate a unique type of understanding to the individual. We might call this a "detached involvement" in the client's problem. Such detachment is necessary to avoid too much sympathy.

As I've said, people who are close to us are biased and can't always put things in proper perspective. They're probably part of the problem. So the professional provides expertise and a unique type of understanding.

WHOM SHOULD WE SEEK COUNSEL FROM, A PASTOR, PSYCHIATRIST, OR PSYCHOLOGIST?

That depends on the nature of our depression, the availability of professional counselors, and the skills of those people. Pastors who are well trained as counselors can provide effective help for minor depressions and referrals to other professionals. Many pastors are not trained to counsel, however. They will know when they've reached the limits of their capabilities in specific situations and will then refer people to more-specialized help. Either a psychologist or a psychiatrist can provide the necessary help for the more severe depressions.

Where medication is necessary, it may be preferable to go directly to a psychiatrist. But clinical psychologists are trained to collaborate with psychiatrists and will call for a consultation if medication is needed. Again, the choice is often determined by the availability of a particular specialist in one's community.

SHOULD WE GO TO A MEDICAL DOCTOR IF WE'RE FEELING DEPRESSED?

If we have a good relationship with a medical doctor, that may be a good place to begin. With knowledge of our background and understanding of our physical condition, he or she would be a good judge of whom we should see next. It should be noted that if a psychologist or psychiatrist feels there is some physical problem in our depression, our doctors should be informed.

DO SOME COUNSELORS SPECIALIZE IN DEPRESSION?

Not really, although some counselors are better at working with depressed people than others. It takes a particular type of understanding and a lot of experience with depression to be good at it. It's possible to be in practice and not see many depressed people or be effective in treating depression. Without that experience, it's difficult to develop the special type of understanding needed.

HOW DOES A DEPRESSED PERSON DETERMINE IF A COUNSELOR IS PROVIDING EFFECTIVE TREATMENT?

It's quite possible that because of the depressed person's bleak outlook, he or she will not be able to judge the counselor's effectiveness. What's important is that the person feel comfortable and trust the therapist. That's critical in the therapeutic relationship. If the person feels uncomfortable, that should be addressed directly to the counselor.

WHERE CAN A PERSON RECEIVE FINANCIAL ASSISTANCE FOR PROFESSIONAL COUNSELING?

The first place is through your health insurance policy. Most medical aid plans now provide assistance for psychological problems, if only for a limited number of sessions. Ask your agent about specific coverage of psychotherapy for depression. In most communities, counseling services are available that charge on a sliding scale related to income. The fees in such cases may be nominal, although few will provide free service.

Interestingly, free service is often not very beneficial, because there's an absence of commitment to the therapeutic process. If a fee is charged, even though it's small, it involves the client to a much greater degree, and the benefit is therefore much greater.

Some churches provide free counseling services to members, so that's an option to explore with your pastor.

IS THERE A DANGER THAT ONE MIGHT SEEK COUNSEL FROM A PASTOR JUST TO AVOID THE COST?

Yes, pastors often get called just because they don't charge for their services. And because their counseling is free, it's tempting to continue going to them longer than we should. Also, some pastors either don't realize or won't admit the limitations of their training in dealing with severe depressions. That could also prolong a depression. Be aware, too, of the tremendous demands on a pastor's time, and be sensitive to his or her need to help many other people as well. If you can pay for the help, employ a professional counselor.

HOW DO I FIND A CHRISTIAN COUNSELOR IN SMALLER OR RURAL COMMUNITIES?

That may be a problem, since counselors don't usually list themselves in the Yellow Pages as being "Christian" (although some do). The obvious first step is to consult your pastor. If he or she doesn't have information, contact a referral agency. Here at the Fuller Graduate School of Psychology, we keep a referral listing, as do the Rosemead Graduate School of Psychology at Biola University and Focus on the Family.[1]

HOW SUCCESSFUL IS MEDICATION IN THE TREATMENT OF DEPRESSION?

Medication is not very helpful in treating the ordinary reactive depressions most of us experience. Its primary use is with the endogenous depressions. The exception would be the occasional use of medication to restore the body's chemical balance after it has been disrupted by a lengthy depression, such as may occur in bereavement. As I have pointed out before, although reactive depression

---

1. Fuller Graduate School of Psychology, 180 N. Oakland Ave., Pasadena, CA 91101, (818) 584-5507; Rosemead School of Psychology, Biola University, 13800 Biola Ave., La Mirada, CA 90639, (213) 944-0351; Focus on the Family, Colorado Springs, CO 80995, (719) 531-3400.

has a psychological cause, it affects the physical system as well. After a long depression, that balance needs to be restored before relief is realized.

Medication is used mostly in the more severe forms of depression, particularly those that have some sort of physical basis. Medicines have revolutionized the treatment of those types of depression.

In treating the very severe, life-threatening forms of depression, medication is essential. It has reduced the need for ECT to the point where the latter is now used infrequently, and it has provided relief from depressive moods for many people.

I spoke recently to a minister friend who has been taking antidepressant medication for more than 12 years for an endogenous depression. He contrasted the first part of his ministry with the second, saying the difference was like that between night and day. For many years after he first became a minister, his mood was constantly depressed. Life was a great burden. After he started taking an antidepressant, his whole attitude changed. He now enjoys the ministry and is much more effective in his work. His body no longer sabotages his mood, and he feels relatively free from the depressions that used to plague him.

Medication may sometimes be used in reactive or psychological depressions that are of long standing, where the body's chemical balance may have been disturbed. The medication helps to give the body a "jump start." However, in long-standing neurotic depressions, antidepressant medication is of little value. The reason is simple: such depressions are not true depressions but problems in living.

WHAT SORTS OF MEDICATION ARE PRESCRIBED?

There are basically two types of medication, tricyclic antidepressants and mono-amine-oxidase inhibitors (known as MAOI's). The tricyclics are given under a variety of trade names and are the most common form of antidepressant. They are frequently used in combination with a tranquilizer to control both anxiety and depression, particularly in agitated depressions.

The second major type of medication, the MAOI's, is used less frequently and normally only after a tricyclic has proved to be ineffective. Because of significant side effects, MAOI's are usually given in a hospital setting, where the individual can be watched carefully. Strict dietary restrictions must be in force. More and more, however, MAOI's are now being used on an outpatient basis with great effectiveness.

What types of side effects occur with these medications?

Some of the general side effects are dry mouth, dizziness, insomnia, and constipation. Only the dry mouth is of real significance, and that often goes away in a week. A number of side effects are unique to different individuals, and even those will occur with varying intensity. If a person can't tolerate the side effects, all that's usually needed is to cut back to a lower dose of the medication, and the body rapidly adjusts to that level. When the side effects disappear, the person can return to the prescribed level.

The side effects are most intense during the first few weeks. The antidepressant drugs, unlike many others, take time before they take effect (up to three weeks). This is good in that it prevents a person from becoming dependent on them. Addictions are not a problem. The most important point to remember is that the benefit lies beyond the side effects. Those needing these drugs should not be put off by the side effects and give up too soon.

What variables contribute to the severity of the side effects?

The key variable is the individual's sensitivity to drugs. People differ in their sensitivity. Some can stand large amounts of a particular medication in their bodies and not notice it at all. Others can hardly bear to take an aspirin.

Another general variable is the degree to which one is involved with life. Someone who is hospitalized for two to three weeks while starting on a medication, for example, tends not to notice the side effects as much as one who is under stress and continuing a normal life's routine.

How soon can results be expected?

There is a slow buildup with the antidepressants. Significant improvement should not be expected sooner than three weeks after the medication is started. For some, it may be a bit longer than that. By the same token, people should never just stop taking antidepressants suddenly. They should be phased out slowly over a period of three weeks or so.

It's often necessary to try several antidepressants before the right one is found; the biochemical disturbance can take many forms, and a different medication is used to treat each one.

IS THERE A TEMPTATION TO OPT FOR MEDICATION OVER PSYCHOTHERAPY AS A QUICK CURE FOR DEPRESSION?

Sometimes there is, but in the case of reactive or psychological depressions, the idea of a quick cure is ill-founded. Medication is of little value in treating them. Sometimes medicine is prescribed to help a person sleep, but since there is no actual physical defect in those depressions, medication can't change anything.

HOW SUCCESSFUL IS ELECTRO-CONVULSIVE THERAPY?

A large percentage of endogenous depressions, including the severe psychotic depressions, respond well to ECT. It brings rapid improvement and is therefore justified when the person is a high suicide risk. Unfortunately, many people avoid this type of treatment because of misconceptions about its use.

WHY IS ECT SUCH A CONTROVERSIAL PROCEDURE?

Fear and misunderstanding are the basis of the controversy. The thought of someone taking control over us, of having a convulsion, is very fear-provoking for many people.

Much of the fear is based on misunderstanding. People don't know exactly what goes on, so they expect the worst, even though ECT is less destructive to the body than having a tooth removed.

In times past, ECT was used on a wide variety of people in mental institutions, sometimes without proper permission and inappropriately. That has left some people with a lingering suspicion based on horror stories they've heard. The media have not been particularly helpful in this regard, tending to perpetuate misconceptions about ECT.

WHAT VARIABLES CONTROL THE EFFECTIVENESS OF ECT?

Several factors help determine the effectiveness of ECT. The severity of the depression is an important variable. The more severe the depression, the more effective is ECT. Also, longstanding depressions tend not to respond to ECT. Age is another important factor. The younger the person, the more effective is the ECT; the older the person, the greater the risk. Often ECT cannot be used on an older person because of hardening of the arteries and the risk of stroke.

ARE THERE INDIVIDUAL DIFFERENCES
IN RESPONSES TO ECT?

We're not sure whether differences in response to ECT are due to individual factors or to differences in the type of depression. It's probably a combination of both, but at this point we can't distinguish between them.

DOES ECT DAMAGE THE BRAIN IN ANY WAY?

There is no evidence that ECT causes any brain damage in healthy people beyond that which occurs normally. Brain cells are dying in all of us every day, and that decay accelerates after about age 30. I must also point out that many people experience unrecognized seizures regularly—daily or even several times a day. Those seizures are much greater than could be induced by any ECT damage. The risk of damage by ECT is negligible when the patient is properly screened and the ECT is administered competently. Fear prevents many people from seeking a very effective treatment for depression.

ARE THERE ANY SIDE EFFECTS TO ECT?

The side effects are minimal, because the treatment is given under an anesthetic and with a muscle relaxant. There's usually a bit of confusion and vagueness immediately after the treatment, but that passes quickly. There is sometimes some memory loss for recent events, but that also lasts only a short time, perhaps the rest of the day. Most people can have ECT on an outpatient basis and go home within a few hours. I should mention, too, that today there are variations in the way ECT is done. It may be necessary to convulse the whole brain, but in many cases only half the brain is convulsed. That reduces memory loss. The ideal is to do as little convulsing as is appropriate for the depression.

N I N E

Caring, Supportive Relationships

A major problem in helping a relative or friend through depression is a lack of knowledge about the subject, as well as a lack of sensitivity. If you're a "helper" to such a person, reading the previous chapters should give you a good deal of insight into how to support that individual. An accurate understanding of the nature and causes of depression is essential to helping someone who is depressed.

The material in this chapter is specifically presented to guide helpers as they seek to give the most effective understanding and support possible to a depressed friend or spouse. It is not designed to take the place of professional help, simply to make you a wiser and more empathetic helper. If you're in close contact with a depressed person, you'll be an important part of the healing process whether you want to be or not.

This chapter has two broad divisions. The first section deals with general questions and answers that apply to anyone you would like to help—friends or family members. The second section relates specifically to helping family members. For information about helping depressed children and adolescents, read chapter 4.

Do depressed people want to talk about their depression?

Very much so, but they don't want to talk to just anybody. They want to talk to someone who will understand and not judge them.

When people are depressed, they're very sensitive to relationships. There may be factors in your relationship that keep the depressed person from exposing too much of his or her inner feelings to you. Sometimes the very closeness of a relationship makes the person uncomfortable with discussing problems. Don't take this personally.

Talking about the depression often results in a sense of relief for the depressed person. Perhaps he or she hasn't yet recognized there's a problem. Or if he or she has recognized it, your being willing to listen at least gets it out in the open. That clears the air and helps communication on the whole depression.

Should you leave a depressed person alone for a while before you offer help?

The help should come right at the beginning. It's easier to get involved earlier rather than later. Remember that depression saps energy and self-esteem, and it interferes with a person's ability or wish to get help. If someone you know shows symptoms of depression but hasn't talked to you about it, show your love and concern by drawing that person aside and gently encouraging him or her to talk to you. Often there's a sense of relief when someone approaches and says, "I can see you're hurting. Why don't you discuss it with me so we can be in this together?" That's all we need sometimes to take the first step toward getting help.

The nature of the help you can offer may change through the different phases of the depression, but the help should always be there, assuming you have the proper rapport with the person. If he or she is a stranger or a distant friend, you should realize you haven't yet earned the right to become involved.

How can I catch the warning signs of depression in someone early enough to prevent it?

It's difficult to catch depression early, because it usually comes on rapidly. By the time you see it, it's fully developed. Reactive depressions, and especially serious psychotic depressions, sometimes come on in a matter of hours, certainly in a few days. You must avoid feeling a failure because you couldn't prevent the depression. If some loss has occurred, the person *needs* to be depressed. The depression will come despite your best intentions. What you do *during* the depression is much more important than trying to prevent or abort it.

WHEN A DEPRESSED PERSON IS RETREATING FROM EVERYONE ELSE, SHOULD I ATTEMPT TO PUSH FOR A CONTACT?

The word *push* is too strong, but you do need to be "assertive" in moving toward him or her. You must make the first approach. If you push too strongly, you'll cause resistance. "Gentle nudging" would perhaps be more appropriate than the idea of pushing. But be prepared for some rejection, and keep coming back.

IN MY FIRST CONTACT WITH A DEPRESSED PERSON, WHAT SHOULD I CONCENTRATE ON?

The most important thing is to communicate understanding and acceptance. The person's encounter with most people will lead him to believe his depression is not acceptable, that he should feel guilty about being depressed, and that he should not really be depressed at all. You can communicate acceptance in a number of ways, but the message you need to send is, "It's all right for you to show your depression to me. It's okay for you to be depressed. Help me understand why you're depressed." This starts an important process toward the healing of the depression.

WHAT'S THE MOST IMPORTANT THING I CAN DO FOR MY DEPRESSED FRIEND OR SPOUSE?

Again, I cannot stress strongly enough the importance of communicating love and acceptance and of avoiding being judgmental.

I'm not saying that being accepting is easy. We have a lot of difficulty accepting someone who is depressed, because we fear the depression will rub off on us or make us feel uncomfortable. But when you are close to a depressed person, you have to accept the reality of the problem. It's there whether you like it or not, and your responsibility is to communicate love and acceptance in whatever way you possibly can.

HOW DO I STRIKE A BALANCE BETWEEN EMPATHY, SYMPATHY, REASSURANCE, AND CONFRONTATION IN RELATING TO SOMEONE WHO IS DEPRESSED?

I seldom see confrontation as helpful. Sometimes it must be done, but only rarely. I prefer *reflecting* rather than *confronting*. In reflecting, you hold up a mirror so feelings can be recognized and accepted by the person.

You can do this effectively by using clarifying questions. Rather than saying, "Well, you're angry, and that's why you're depressed; just get rid of your anger and you won't be depressed anymore," you can say, "Don't you think there might be a large amount of anger in what you feel? Tell me about this anger." By approaching it this way, you are recognizing that the person's emotions are not always deliberate, that he or she might not intend to be angry, self-pitying, or whatever, even though that's the case. This gives your friend a chance to own up to and accept those emotions rather than build up resistance to judgmental confrontations.

Empathy, the communication of understanding and acceptance, is the most helpful attitude. Give reassurance: "Although I can't personally experience your depression, I'm in this with you. I'm not going to leave you alone. I won't abandon you." That's what you need to convey.

IS THERE ANY PLACE FOR CONFRONTATION IN THIS KIND OF RELATIONSHIP?

Obviously, there is a place for confrontation in real relationships. But I would caution against confrontation as a general style. Most times it is damaging, because it's usually done with an element of anger and frustration. How can you, an outsider, confront when you don't know all the details? You only see your side of the issue. We want to rush in because something looks so obvious from our perspective, but we don't always understand the full context. It is far better to hold back and first try to be understanding. That earns you the right to confront later.

A qualified exception would be during the recovery phase of the depression, as I've mentioned before. Then a low-key confrontation, a gentle prodding and pushing, may be helpful.

SHOULD I BE SYMPATHETIC AND TRY TO ENTER THE DEPRESSED PERSON'S MOOD, OR SHOULD I TRY TO CHEER HIM OR HER UP?

The key word again is *empathy*. Don't be too sympathetic. Don't enter the individual's mood to the extent that you begin to feel depressed yourself. That doesn't help you or the other person. But do communicate understanding and acceptance. He or she wants someone who can see the loss from his or her perspective and in that context give reassurance.

Don't give advice, whatever you do. Some people feel they haven't done anything helpful unless they've given advice. Don't criticize. Be prepared to listen, and be determined to understand what the person is feeling.

WHY DO WE SEEM TO HAVE THE NEED, AS SUPPORTIVE FRIENDS AND RELATIVES, TO GIVE ADVICE?

As friends and loved ones, we want to be helpful, so we resort to advice giving. This approach is based on the erroneous idea that our friends or relatives have no reason to be depressed. There's always a reason for depression. I'm not suggesting that all depression is appropriate, but if we grant people the right to be depressed when it is, we can relieve a lot of our anxiety and be more supportive.

SHOULD I TRY TO TALK A DEPRESSED PERSON OUT OF HIS OR HER DEPRESSION?

Whatever else you do, do not try to talk the person out of being depressed. It's common for someone who is depressed and who reveals these feelings to someone else to get a response that says something like, "Come on now. You don't have any reason to be depressed. Why don't you just shake yourself out of it and forget about your feelings?" Such statements are callous and unfeeling. They only make the depressed person feel worse.

HOW MUCH DOES IT HELP TO "IDENTIFY" WITH A PERSON WHO IS DEPRESSED?

The reason many people pull away when they're depressed is that they fear others will not identify with them in their depression. They think others won't accept them in their depressed state (very much like the withdrawal of many cancer patients when their disease or treatment causes changes in their bodies). It's not so much that they want to be alone, but they want to avoid being with people who won't accept their depression. It's really a protective move on their part. The more you can identify with someone else's depression, without becoming depressed yourself, the greater help you can be.

WHEN THE BIBLE SAYS "WEEP WITH THOSE WHO WEEP," DOES IT MEAN I SHOULD TRY TO SHARE THEIR FEELINGS OF DEPRESSION?

It doesn't mean you should also become depressed. That verse is a call to understanding, not to taking on another person's pain. For some reason, our guilt mechanisms won't allow us to be supportive and understanding to a depressed person without wanting to become depressed with them. This is one of the reasons we avoid depressed people. Our proneness to sympathy triggers the same pain in us.

In "weeping with those who weep," remember that while you may share their feelings, and may indeed weep because they're in pain, you're only going to aggravate their depression if you become depressed as well. You must get involved with their feelings but retain an objective understanding.

Keep in mind that this is their depression, not yours. And you are not Christ. Only He suffered for us and bore our sicknesses on the cross. The best you can do is try to understand.

SHOULD I HELP SOMEONE WHO IS DEPRESSED TO CONCENTRATE ON IDENTIFYING THE LOSS, OR SHOULD I JUST BE AN IMPARTIAL LISTENER?

It's important that the depressed person identify the loss. In providing a listening ear, you can help him or her communicate this loss and develop some understanding of the events that caused it. The key to most good therapy is to help a client discover what's causing the problem, because when that discovery is made, it's so much more meaningful and so much easier to take the corrective steps.

Your role is to facilitate the discovery of the loss or the understanding of the disturbed physiology. Of course, if you see something obvious that's being overlooked, you should present this to the person. In doing that, present it in the form of a question rather than a dogmatic statement. For instance, ask, "Do you think you are clinging to your past job because you're afraid you can't get another?" That's better than saying, "I think you're just afraid you'll never get another job."

Using a question lets the person reflect on it. If the notion is rejected, you can come back a little later and ask the question again. That way you can help him or her come to realize the significance of what you are suggesting.

Is there a place for probing?

Active listening is the key technique here, not cross-questioning or probing. That means you are constantly checking out what you're hearing by reflecting it back to your friend in a process of clarification: "Now is this what you mean?" "Are you saying that having your spouse walk out on you represents this to you, or are you worried about what the children have lost rather than what you've lost?" In active listening, you are clarifying things for yourself, but more importantly, you're clarifying them for the other person.

Besides listening, are there other basic points I should concentrate on when I'm trying to be supportive?

Beyond helping the depressed person identify the losses that have been suffered, or in the case of endogenous depression ensuring that the appropriate treatment is obtained, you can help in exploring the full implications of the loss. The person needs to get beyond the "global" reasons (I lost my job) to just what that means to him or her. There may be many associated losses such as the loss of self-respect or the respect of a parent or friend. Once the person has that more-complete awareness, he or she will be able to grieve all the losses fully and finally get on with life.

You also need to support the person's course of medication. Depressed people tend not to want to take their medication.

You need not be a professional counselor to do these things, but you may disqualify yourself as a helpful counselor if you become too personally and emotionally involved with the depression. If the person's loss triggers in you too many insecure feelings, you should back off. That's why, in our culture, it's more efficient and often more effective to get professional help.

What is the single most dangerous error I can make in counseling someone who is depressed?

Making that person feel guilty about being depressed. On the other hand, if you're able to break the cycle of guilt, you'll go a long way toward alleviating and shortening a depression. We reduce guilt by repeatedly reassuring the depressed person that we understand and accept his or her state of mind. As long as we're consistent in showing love and acceptance, we are not aggravating the depression.

HOW DO I RECOGNIZE SUICIDAL TENDENCIES IN A DEPRESSED PERSON?

It's not always easy, because if people are intending suicide, they often become secretive, withdraw, and won't talk to anyone. On the other hand, there's frequently a "cry for help" in some action. If they repeatedly talk about taking their lives and you don't pay attention, they can very easily do it.

Contrary to myth, it's not true that if a person talks about suicide, he or she won't do it. Many people who have committed suicide have talked about it for a long time before acting, and no one paid any attention. Many make statements such as, "I wish I were dead," "I can't take it anymore," "My family would be better off without me," or "I want out."

Some even tell a friend about a plan to kill themselves before they do it. If a friend or spouse talks like that, take it seriously. Immediate steps are necessary to prevent any further damage. If your friend or spouse wants to talk about suicide, by all means encourage him or her to do so. A depressed person needs the freedom to talk about those feelings.

If you feel a person is depressed but not talking about suicide, ask him or her to express thoughts about death. Watch for signs of secretiveness, hostility, or aggression. The suicidal person often has a lot of hostility that can't be expressed. Anything you can do to help the person talk about this anger will be helpful.

HOW CAN I BEGIN TO MOTIVATE SOMEONE WHO IS DEPRESSED?

The motivation, not surprisingly, comes out of this supportive relationship. Depressed people are not motivated to seek help, and the deeper the depression, the less they will seek it. The depression itself destroys motivation. Motivation is created and builds as they feel there is understanding and reassurance. When you make yourself available to listen in an understanding way, you begin to build motivation.

How do I recognize the time to stop listening and begin to give positive suggestions?

You never stop listening. The question should be, "When do I add some positive suggestions to my listening?" That depends on the severity of the depression and the stage at which you find the person. During the recovery phase, you can be a lot more assertive and directive. It's a safe time to do that. The mistake is attempting it in the early stages of the depression, when the person is not yet ready to respond.

It's not easy for a lay person to know exactly when the turning point occurs. One important clue is when the depression shows some little signs of lifting. Perhaps there are moments when the depression is not as intense, or the person may laugh for a moment. Now you can be a bit more positive and directive in what you say—but never stop listening.

What can I do to short-circuit a friend or relative's depression?

The notion of "short-circuiting" always implies that you do something to prevent the depressive process from running its full course. When you try to do that by, for instance, getting the person to immediately get a new cat to replace one that died, you invariably aggravate the depression.

In rare cases, you might make just the right comment to give the person the perspective he or she needs to resolve the depression before it gets too deep. But that would be more a matter of luck than skill. We shouldn't be so afraid of sadness. It plays an important role in developing maturity.

There are certainly no general rules I could give to help short-circuit a depression. A more important emphasis is to allow the sufferer the freedom to experience a full and appropriate depression. That's the quickest way to bring healing.

Love, acceptance, and understanding can work miracles to speed up our grief. An example of this is a couple who came to see me because of the husband's deep depression. As I worked with them, it became obvious that he had some legitimate reasons for his depressions. In treatment, all I did was help the wife to become more accepting and understanding of his losses. Within days, the man was out of his severe depression.

You see, he suffered more than just the original loss. It had been compounded by the loss of his wife's love, acceptance, and understanding, which was perpetuating the depression. You can't go wrong by giving loving support.

IF I HAVEN'T EXPERIENCED SIGNIFICANT DEPRESSION MYSELF, DOES THAT DISQUALIFY ME FROM BEING EFFECTIVE AND SUPPORTIVE?

No, it doesn't, as long as it doesn't make you less understanding. Unfortunately, people who haven't experienced a major depression are not always understanding. If you've never experienced much pain, it's difficult to understand what it's like to be in a lot of pain. If you haven't experienced depression, it's hard to know what it is to be depressed. But being a good listener will quickly teach you, and it's the better way to learn.

IF I'VE HAD MY OWN DEPRESSION, SHOULD I DESCRIBE MY EXPERIENCES?

There are times when describing your own depression experiences can be helpful, but avoid doing so with an attitude of, "Well, I've been depressed, too, and it didn't affect me as much as it seems to affect you." You may think you are helping the other person by putting his or her experience in the perspective of your depression, but this self-glorifying approach only increases guilt and depression.

Discuss your experiences sensitively, always keeping the focus on the other person. An attitude of "We're all in the same boat" is helpful. What's important is to work at building rapport, where the depressed person feels he or she can open up to you in trust. You must establish a base of acceptance, which is granted by the depressed person, before you can begin describing your own past.

AM I IN DANGER OF BECOMING DEPRESSED AGAIN BY HELPING SOMEONE ELSE IN DEPRESSION?

Not at all. As I've mentioned several times, depression is *not* contagious in this sense. The particular reasons for your own depression may be quite different from those of the other person, so you're not likely to become depressed just by being helpful. If anything, you are likely to be more understanding and accepting of your own experiences. You do, of course, need to avoid becoming sympathetic. That could suck you down into depression. By remaining objective and reminding yourself that this is not your depression, you can avoid that pitfall.

HOW DO I ENCOURAGE SOMEONE WHO IS DEPRESSED TO CONSULT A PROFESSIONAL THERAPIST?

If the person is not your spouse, you first need to consult with those closest to him or her—a spouse or significant close relative. You all need to be in agreement on what action should be recommended. It is far better if the direction comes from those closest to the depressed person. You could make the suggestion to them and encourage them to follow up on it.

If you're the closest person or there is no one but you, you need to come right out with it in a straightforward manner. Be sure to put it in the context of your love and care for your friend or relative; don't present it in a critical or judgmental way.

IS THERE A DANGER THAT THE DEPRESSED PERSON WILL BECOME ANGRY AT THE SUGGESTION?

That's a risk you have to take. If there is an angry response, you need to work through that anger together. Receive it—don't draw away or become offended. Engage the anger: "Well, why does it make you angry to have me caring for you this much? Is it because you don't realize how depressed you are?" In this way you can drain a lot of the anger and work it through to a point where he or she is ready to accept your suggestion.

CAN I HELP SOMEONE OVERCOME CONCERNS FROM THE PAST THAT ARE TRIGGERING DEPRESSION?

You can do a lot in this direction. You can't help your friend or spouse get over every problem, but there's much you can do to help him or her bear concerns more courageously. The early traumas of life tend to set us up with memories that can re-create, at some later time, all the painful feelings of those experiences. They then haunt us and often cause depression.

The most important thing you can do is to encourage the person to talk about them. The more he or she can do that, the more rapidly some perspective on these early events can develop. Just by discussing them with you, he or she may gain some fantastic insights and come to an "Aha!" experience. It all begins to fall into place then.

This listening is critical to helping someone overcome early traumas that may be bothering him or her. I once counseled a young woman who a year earlier had had an abortion. She came to consult me because she was severely depressed, but she didn't really know why. As I explored with her what was going on in her life, she began to think a lot about the abortion. She hadn't wanted it, but her husband had insisted. She realized it was wrong at the time, but to please her husband she had gone through with it, and now she regretted it.

As we talked and she said what had happened, she interjected, "You know what has suddenly occurred to me? There's nothing I can do to change that event from my past." Her face lit up. That idea freed her. She had taken God's forgiveness and was willing to move ahead with her life. By the end of the session, we had broken the back of her depression.

We can't change history, and we can't always just forget the past. But we can remove from our memories the power to re-create hurts in the present. It was this belief that freed her to give up her depression.

IF RE-CREATING EMOTIONS FROM THE PAST CAN LEAD TO DEPRESSION IN THE PRESENT, CAN WE TURN IT AROUND AND HELP A PERSON OUT OF DEPRESSION BY RE-CREATING PLEASANT EMOTIONS ASSOCIATED WITH THE PAST?

Yes, we can help by reminding depressed people of pleasant past experiences. But that's only helpful during the recovery phase of a depression. During the early phase, when they're still going into a depression, the depression distorts their outlook, including memory. By drawing attention to the good things in the past, we may just be accentuating their awareness of the bad things in the present.

Once they have started to recover and are beginning to show signs of normality, focusing on pleasant experiences and emotions from the past can help put things in a better perspective. By remembering what it's like to feel good, they begin to feel more hopeful.

HOW DO I HELP KEEP A DEPRESSED PERSON FROM TURNING TO ALCOHOL AS A WAY OF COMBATING DEPRESSION?

If proper treatment is being provided, there is little tendency for the individual to turn to alcohol. Alcohol is primarily a tranquilizer, used to alleviate anxiety. The depression itself does not make one prone to alcohol; it's the anxiety associated with the depression that causes it. So anything you can do to alleviate anxiety will help to reduce the need for alcohol. A minor tranquilizer could be given. But the best antidote for anxiety that I know is to be surrounded by loving, caring, and accepting families and friends.

How can I be positive in my Christian influence on my friend or spouse without appearing to be superspiritual or holier-than-thou?

Just be yourself. Don't put on spiritual airs or play the superior game. But there are certain values and perspectives that, as Christians, we have to remind each other of. It's the attitude with which we do this that avoids giving the impression we are superspiritual or holier-than-thou. The most positive thing we can do as Christians, and the most positive influence we can bring to bear, is captured in the concept of Christian love. If that's the context of your concern, you need not fear the reaction. You will fulfill your responsibilities as a Christian in a beneficial way.

Is there any effective way to help an aged friend or relative cope with depression?

People who are nearing the end of life and who become depressed need two things above all else, *structure* and *reassurance*.

I use the term *structure* in a broad sense. When people reach old age, their memories don't function as well as before, so they need to know that everything is in its place. For an older man, it may be that in his workshop he needs to have his tools in the proper place, where he can put his hands on them easily. For a woman, it's knowing that a particular pan is always in its special place. This is needful physical structure.

Older folks also need structure psychologically. Make sure they have emotional and social structure. Don't change the pattern of things unnecessarily. Set up a regular routine. Often there's a desire to take a depressed elderly person out of his or her regular environment, but that often causes confusion.

Not long ago, I saw a well-meaning adult son insist that his aged and depressed mother come to live with him in California. She had lived all her life in the East. He thought the change of environment would help her. Needless to say, her depression got worse. When the son consulted with me, my first recommendation was to put her back in her structured and familiar environment. She is much more likely to be able to cope with her depression in that familiar structure than out of it.

The second thing an aged person needs is reassurance. The tendency to avoid depressed persons is accentuated when the person is older. This withdrawal and avoidance, especially by family members, will aggravate the depression. Give him or her reassurance. Provide as much love as you can show. This is essential for recovery; it prevents the development of other losses.

Can a Husband Effectively Counsel His Wife, or a Wife Her Husband?

Couples need to accept that there's a limit to what counseling can be done between spouses. You can't be everything to one another, and I encourage couples not to try counseling each other. Because of the intimate relationship between them, there is often too much personal and emotional investment in what the spouse is thinking or doing. You can't remain impartial and detached. Just accepting that limitation can go a long way toward avoiding the guilt of not being able to help. It also frees your spouse to seek counsel with someone else.

Having said that, I also realize much can be done by one spouse to help another. I find my own wife to be extremely helpful as a friend and confidante. And it gets better as you get older. As you build a mature relationship, your ability to help each other increases.

I'm Frustrated in Trying to Find the Cause of My Wife's Depression. Should I Keep Probing?

Stay in a listening mode and you'll never make a mistake! You see, the depression may be endogenous, having a biochemical basis. That means there's no psychological cause. It may be an early symptom of an illness or a disease. If you keep probing too much, you may just cause more confusion. That will intensify the depression.

How Much Impact Does My Reaction to My Spouse's Depression Have on His or Her Overcoming It Quickly?

In the severe endogenous depressions, your reaction is not likely to have that much effect. The problem is more physiological, more internal to the individual. In the reactive depressions, however—especially in the recovery phase, where there's a lot of potential for a person to return to the depression—it can be harmful. I've known many instances where just getting the spouse to be more accepting of the depression has greatly helped the person to recover.

I recall a particular couple where the husband had been depressed for many months. His business wasn't doing well, so he was in a continuous state of loss and was depressed most of the time. He couldn't talk to his wife about his problems, because she had shut out communication to protect herself from becoming depressed. He didn't force the issue, as he didn't want her to become depressed, either. So he kept it all to himself. I was able to prepare her so she could receive what he wanted to say without becoming depressed. Just being able to share his problems with her helped to lift his depression.

The wonderful thing was that as soon as his depression lifted, he was able to do something about restoring his business. He had been caught in a vicious cycle. He wasn't doing effective sales work because of his depression, and that was hurting his business, so he became more depressed. Being able to share his depression with his wife and have her accept his feelings and cooperate with him freed him to be more effective in his work. As a result, he was able to get his business out of the low spot it had been in.

HOW CAN I COPE WITH THE FRUSTRATION OF NOT BEING ABLE TO HELP MY SPOUSE OUT OF HIS OR HER DEPRESSION?

You need to realize that helping your spouse is beyond your resources. You're disqualified from being helpful to some extent because of your relationship. In fact, you may be part of the cause of the depression, in which case you need to stand aside. Your anger and frustration will only increase your spouse's guilt at being depressed. A mate's role is primarily one of support. The main therapeutic work needs to be done by a professional.

SHOULD I GO AS FAR AS FORCING MY SPOUSE TO SEE A COUNSELOR?

In very severe depressions, the person won't want to seek help. You will need to exert control in such a situation. Of course you shouldn't resort to force until you've exhausted all other means of reasoning and persuasion. Point out that the depression is not only destructive to him or her, but to everyone around as well. Only if everything else fails should you use force to obtain professional help. If you consult a professional psychologist or psychiatrist, your legal rights to enforce treatment will be explained.

I FEEL A GROWING RESENTMENT OVER THE FACT THAT MY WIFE HAS TO TALK TO SOMEONE ELSE TO RESOLVE HER DEPRESSION.

I can understand that feeling. It seems like an intrusion into your privacy and the intimacy of your relationship. This feeling often arises because we feel we should be all things to our spouses, that we should be able to resolve all problems privately. Up to a point, we can. But a major depression is another matter.

The resentment you feel may arise because of what you're saying to yourself: *If I were the proper kind of husband (wife), I would be able to help him (her) more* or *Who can help her (him) better than I can? I know her (him) better than anyone else.* You need to realize that the depression may be a symptom of an illness, or that the losses suffered are so severe that professional help is needed. Concentrate on giving love and being supportive and understanding.

HOW CAN I AVOID MAKING MY SPOUSE FEEL MORE GUILTY THAN HE OR SHE ALREADY FEELS?

The most important way is to be accepting of the depression. If you communicate any resistance to it, any feeling of being deprived as a result of it, you're going to increase the guilt. People who are depressed do not want to be (although paradoxically, if the depression lasts a long time, they find it difficult to give it up). If your spouse realizes his or her depression is causing you pain, the guilt will be intensified.

WHAT CHANGES IN HOUSEHOLD ROUTINE COULD EASE A DEPRESSION?

The change I would suggest is that you remove unnecessary responsibility. If it's the wife who is depressed, provide some help with the cooking, the housework, or in taking care of the children. You should modify the expectations of everyone in the house to avoid increasing the burden felt by the spouse. To demand full normal performance is totally unreasonable.

Other changes that can help include providing adequate stimulation to the spouse. He or she may be depressed because of lack of variety—nothing interesting or exciting is taking place. Provide a change of routine occasionally. Take your spouse to dinner, for example. That offers a change and removes responsibility as well.

SHOULD I SEEK TO KEEP THE HOUSE QUIET, OR SHOULD I LET THINGS RUN PRETTY MUCH AS USUAL?

Keep things as normal as you possibly can. To make too many adjustments may reinforce the depression by communicating to the depressed person that he or she is disrupting the normal routine. Maintaining routine will help to create a sense of safety and security.

WILL THE RESPONSIBILITIES A SPOUSE FEELS BE ENOUGH TO ACTIVATE HIM OR HER?

No, they won't. The very depression that is the cause of the problem also distorts your spouse's perception of his or her responsibilities. This is especially true in severe depressions where, for example, a mother may not realize the responsibility she has toward her child who needs care. You must gently, lovingly, and understandingly reason with your spouse to convince him or her to keep going.

HOW CAN I HELP MY SPOUSE GET GOING IN THE MORNING?

First, give lots of supportive love. Make sure you don't communicate any aggravation or irritation. Keep some pressure on by explaining clearly how important it is that he or she get up and get going. Give reasons for getting up. Don't assume that because you've said it once, it's understood. Remind your spouse again and again how important it is for him or her to get up, to keep going, to avoid letting his or her bodily system go down unnecessarily.

Don't demand anything, however. Don't invent things to be done. It only creates conflict. I know of some who set up games with their spouses by inventing things to do. The depressed spouse will see through this and resist it. The most important reason to give for getting up is that some energy, some activity, is important in helping the recovery period.

MY HUSBAND'S DEPRESSION IS PUTTING US IN A REAL FINANCIAL SQUEEZE. HOW CAN I COPE WITH THAT ON TOP OF EVERYTHING ELSE?

It's very disturbing when a depression drains the financial resources of a family. It creates more losses. What you need to do is seek assistance. Make sure you're getting all the help you can from your medical insurance and that the treating professional knows what's going on. Perhaps you need to change from an expensive therapist to a community-based clinic where you can pay on a sliding scale based on income.

Above all, you have to remind yourself about priorities. I've known wives to complain about their husband's depression and what it's costing for medication and therapy, and then go out and buy some relatively unimportant but expensive things. This is true of men as well. They may go out and buy a new car, all the while complaining about what their wife's treatment is costing. You must face your priorities and make sure they're balanced. Your spouse's happiness should take priority over other claims on your finances.

I FEAR MY HUSBAND'S DEPRESSION WILL DEEPEN TO THE POINT THAT HE WON'T BE ABLE TO PROVIDE FOR US FINANCIALLY. HOW CAN I AVOID LETTING THIS ANXIETY ADD TO HIS DEPRESSION?

You need to get some help in keeping that anxiety down. Talk to your pastor or your doctor. Find someone to share your feelings with. Trying to carry them within yourself is a sure way of communicating your pain to your spouse.

In my practice, if I have a husband who is deeply depressed, early in the process I will invite the wife to come as well. I realize what a burden the depression imposes on her. She needs to talk about her reaction to it and how she's handling her anxiety so that I can help her reduce it. You, likewise, need to find ways of keeping your own anxiety to a minimum.

IS MY DEPRESSED HUSBAND LIKELY TO HURT ME OR THE CHILDREN?

Not really. Depression itself is not a dangerous disorder, nor does it create any danger. In fact, it's quite the reverse. Your spouse is likely to become passive and will retreat from conflict rather than become aggressive toward family members. There is nothing you need fear when a spouse is depressed.

HOW CAN I HELP MY CHILDREN COPE WITH MY SPOUSE'S DEPRESSION?

Children are remarkably resilient. They have the ability to detach themselves, if necessary, to protect themselves. Most of the time you won't have to worry about how your children are handling it. But your children's reaction to your spouse could aggravate the depression. You need to sit down alone with them and explain the nature of the problem. The more information they have, the more understanding and accepting they can be. Then encourage them not to be judgmental but to emphasize acceptance and love.

SHOULD I ENCOURAGE SOCIAL CONTACTS WITH OUR FRIENDS EVEN THOUGH MY SPOUSE DOESN'T WANT THEM?

You can encourage ongoing contact with close friends, and certainly other family members, who are accepting of the depression. Maintain contact with them as much as you can. But don't expose your spouse to more-distant friends who may not accept the depression or who will be callous and misunderstanding. Strangers should be kept far away. Your depressed spouse will not be able to build new relationships.

HOW CAN I BEGIN TO GET MY SPOUSE SOCIALLY ACTIVE AGAIN?

Encouraging social activity should only be considered during the recovery phase. It won't be helpful to force social activity during the earlier phases, and certainly not during the deepest part of depression. In the recovery phase, begin by inviting close, understanding friends who haven't been around for a while to renew contact. Start with those nearest you, and slowly expand the circle outward as your depressed spouse builds social tolerance. A few good experiences with others builds the depressed person's confidence. If the experience is bad, you may have to wait a bit before trying another. Of course, I'm assuming contact has been maintained with immediate family members throughout, where there is a greater level of acceptance.

SHOULD I TELL OUR PARENTS THAT MY SPOUSE IS RECEIVING TREATMENT FROM A PSYCHOLOGIST OR PSYCHIATRIST?

As a general rule, I believe in total honesty. No secrets! I would encourage openness wherever possible. I don't see any value in concealing the fact that your spouse is seeking help, although some may have to make an exception where parents are not understanding. Usually, though, the more people who know about it, the more love and encouragement your spouse can receive from them.

We also need to break down the stigma attached to seeking help. Not only should we not be ashamed about this, but it's even a mark of maturity and courage that we're willing to expose our needs and seek help from someone outside the family.

CONCLUSION

Having read through the core of this material on depression, you have seen two major themes. (1) Depression is often an appropriate emotion or a symptom of some biological disturbance. (2) Communicating understanding and acceptance is the key to the effective support of a depressed person. The second theme clearly rests on the first, for if you won't accept depression as an inevitable experience of life, you can't give the empathetic support that will help to resolve the depression.

I would encourage you, as a concerned helper, to persist in developing an understanding of depression. But more importantly, I urge you to work at communicating understanding and acceptance of a depressed friend or relative in the context of love. That is your Christian responsibility, and it can only be achieved completely through the power of Christ. You will need all the help He can give you.

Section III

Growth Experiences through Depression

In this last section, three well-known Christian writers describe their personal bouts with depression. They also reveal lessons they learned as a result, along with the ways God provided for them. My prayer is that their stories will encourage and inspire you with the assurance that God knows and cares about your pain, and that there is an end to the suffering.

T E N

Joni Eareckson Tada

J oni's story is well known. The diving accident that paralyzed her from shoulders to toes, and the subsequent development of a vibrant faith and ministry, have been the focus of two books and a film. She has also personalized her experiences in hundreds of speaking engagements.

In this account, Joni describes her experiences with depression, from the severe, suicidal depressions shortly after her accident to the recurring threats of depression from the frustrations of day-to-day living with a permanent and massive loss. This material is taken from an interview recorded in June 1980, when Joni had been flat in bed for a couple of weeks and was battling with frustration, claustrophobia, and an increased sense of helplessness.

Joni's testimony to God's steadfast working in her life through her accident and subsequent depressions will confirm the principle that God's purposes are good, and that He will provide a way of growth through the most devastating circumstances if we trust Him.

I grew up in the west Baltimore suburbs in a family where depression really wasn't common. We always enjoyed good health and good family relationships. Very rarely were there severe arguments. I'm not sure if it was because of the joy that existed in my family or the fact that my parents are very easygoing and discipline was a structural, commonplace part of our household. In either case, I don't remember struggling with severe depression when I was a youngster.

As I went through my teenage years, however, I, like most teens, faced a time of inadequacy and struggling with my self-worth and self-esteem—a time of personal identity crisis. I found Christ as my Savior when I was a sophomore in high school, and that gave me a deep sense of belonging and alleviated many problems, at least on the surface.

But in 1967, when I was ready to graduate from high school, I suffered a traumatic and life-changing injury.

My sister Kathy and I were swimming in Chesapeake Bay on a hot July day. I dove into what turned out to be very shallow water and immediately struck bottom. The impact snapped my vertebrae, severed my spinal column, and in an instant I was left paralyzed, without the use of my hands or my legs.

In the first couple of months after my injury, I didn't have much of a problem with depression. I suppose it was because I enjoyed the novelty of what it meant to be in a hospital and have people visit, send me flowers, and what not. I also didn't realize the full nature of my injury. But as the weeks of my hospitalization slipped into months, I sank deeper and deeper into depression.

The depression became even more severe as I discovered the permanency of my paralysis. When this realization began to sink in, I discovered a deep and despairing sense of hopelessness. No hope of ever walking again. No hope of ever using my hands again. No hope of enjoying a marriage with children and all those things I had so dreamed about as a young girl. I wanted to end my life, and the frustration I felt at not even being able to do that only intensified my depression. I was so desperate, I begged one of my friends to help me end it all.

What seemed to make my depression even worse was the way I had held in my true feelings for so long during those weeks of hospitalization. Because I didn't want to drive my family or friends away with bitterness or anger about my situation, I hadn't expressed the quiet rage I was feeling.

Slowly, over the months after my hospitalization, I began to share myself with a small, intimate circle of friends. Once I saw their acceptance and love, a lot of the bitterness melted, and that helped me deal more honestly with my depression.

First I began to understand that it's okay to be depressed. In fact, it was part of the life cycle that David, Moses, and Solomon went through.

Then I began to reconstruct real hope from the Word of God. For instance, one thing that really helped me in the middle of my hopelessness and depression was to know that at least I had the very real hope of one day having a body that worked. Of having hands that would hug and feet that would run. Not necessarily an angel costume, but a glorified body, much like the kind Christ had after His resurrection. He walked with His disciples, ate with them, and did very earthly, human things. It gave me a great deal of comfort to know I hadn't been left alone in that hopelessness, that God had provided the answer by His promise of a new body.

A part of the quiet rage I experienced was anger against God. Inwardly and very quietly, I raved and ranted against Him in my spirit. I think it's better to get angry at God than to walk away from Him. It's better to honestly confront our feelings and let Him know this is how we feel—this is awful, my pillow is wet from all my tears, I'm sick and tired of this, and I can't stand it one more minute. That's better than passing on a Colgate smile, gritting your teeth, and pretending you're not hurting.

Admittedly, I felt some guilt afterward. But I was encouraged by reading examples from the Psalms. In so many, David rants and raves and just can't understand what God is doing, but nonetheless, at the end, there is invariably a ray of hope—"Yet will I trust in Thee."

The example of Jeremiah was also an encouragement. He was terribly depressed amid the horror, the battle, the invasion, the cruelty and mockery that was going on. Yet Jeremiah says that God's lovingkindness never ceases, His mercies are new every morning, His compassions never fail, therefore I will trust Him. Jeremiah chose to believe what he knew to be true about God rather than relying on some assessment based on his current circumstances.

These examples of people in Scripture who were very real, very honest, and very human were a great encouragement. They got angry and upset and depressed. They weren't plaster saints, but real men and women who hurt and were angry and yet nonetheless held on to what they knew to be true about God from history and from His Word.

And that is essentially how I dealt with my guilt. I found I was not alone in my feelings of depression and anger. The Bible was full of people who were terribly confused and upset, yet they hung on to their God. I realized these emotions were part of what it means to be human, and that to feel guilty about feelings of depression was really to feel guilty about being human.

I had to deal with the whole matter of my helplessness, too. Here I was, a girl who had been very athletic, who enjoyed sports, who loved horseback riding and swimming, now being reduced to total dependency on others. I had this terrible sense of helplessness, a feeling that my life from here on out would revolve totally around other people's schedules, other people's time and attention. This contributed to my depression, of course, but in time, through sharing myself with the others in this small, intimate group, I began to understand it's okay to be dependent.

I also began to understand I was not a helpless victim of circumstances. God has declared in His Word that He is sovereign and protective, and that in His personal concern for me, all circumstances are fitted into a pattern for good. I was not the brunt of some monstrous trick conceived in heaven. I was not a pawn in a chess match or in the middle of an arm-wrestling match between God and Satan. God assured me He had reasons for this, and though I certainly couldn't understand all of them, at least I could rest on His character and nature. He promised in His Word that all this was going to work out not only for my good, but also for His glory, and I could relax in the truth and love and justice of His character—which, of course, is best explained by the cross.

It comforted me a good deal in my depression to look at Jesus and know that because He had been impaled and paralyzed on that cross, He knew exactly how I felt. I had a Savior who had been tempted and tested and tried in every way like myself.

Then, of course, my feelings of worthlessness contributed to my depression as well. Not being able to use my hands, I really grappled with a sense of inadequacy, of unproductiveness. What could I contribute to society? Was there anything I could do that would be of worth or meaning?

When I had been on my feet, I used the usual yardsticks to gauge what I considered usefulness, productivity, or achievement: material wealth, career opportunities, successful marriages. A jock will measure you by your athletic ability, a seminary student by your brains. But after my injury, all those yardsticks were shattered. I had to find a whole new way of looking at what was really productive, meaningful, and worthwhile.

Slowly I began to see that what would give me a worthwhile position in society and a sense of self-esteem was perhaps different from the values society had once placed on me. I couldn't measure up any longer. My goodness, if I went shopping, I would look at a mannequin and envy her because clothes hung better on her than they did on me sitting in a wheelchair!

I had to set aside all those societal standards and take hold again of what I knew to be true about myself from the Word of God. And God has said that what really counts in eternity is my response to my situations. I may not have been responsible for getting myself into this wheelchair, but I am responsible for how I respond to it. Even if it means tears and boredom—or now, yes, even deep depression—God has called me to be responsible.

God knows our frame. He bottles our tears; He binds up the wounds of the brokenhearted and takes no pleasure in our pain. But nonetheless, He calls us to be responsible. My sense of worth came from knowing that what counted for eternity was the way I responded in these circumstances no matter how discouraging, irritating, or frustrating they might be. That's what was winning me a rich reward in heaven and a changed life here on earth. The cultivation of a Christlike character by responding responsibly to my injury gave me a sense of worth.

Of course, I can hear someone say, "Well, it's fine for Joni to talk that way. After all, she has impact on millions of lives with her books, movies, art, and speaking engagements. Of course she has a sense of worth." But let me point out that I was in my wheelchair for eight years before I was even approached about that first book. I had spent most of those years working through these various struggles, long before I had any popularity.

One of the by-products of all these components of depression was strong feelings of self-pity. I worked my way through them in two ways. First, from a human perspective, I found that sitting in a corner and crying for myself wasn't making me or anyone around me happier, so I'd better get on the stick and shape up. That was one approach I took, and it certainly helped.

The other approach was through the Word of God again. I remember the incident where Peter was beginning to get real upset because it seemed Jesus was showing some favoritism to John. Peter confronts Jesus and says, "Look, this is what you're doing with John, and it seems to me I'm getting the worst end of the deal."

And Jesus answers, "Peter, what is that to thee? Follow thou me." In other words, "It's none of your business what I'm doing in John's life. Your business is simply to keep your eye on Me." One might have thought Jesus would say, "There, there, Peter. Everything's going to be okay," and patted him on the head or wrapped His arms around him. Maybe doing that would have fostered Peter's self-pity; I don't know. But instead Jesus uses a stern rebuke. In a sense He shakes His finger at Peter and says, "Look. What's the issue here, Peter? You should trust in Me. Don't compare your lot in life to somebody else's. Get your focus where it belongs—on the author and finisher of your faith."

When I took a long, hard look at that portion of Scripture in John 21, I saw I was making the same mistake as Peter. I was, in a sense, comparing my lot in life to that of everybody on their feet, even mannequins! And I'd come out losing, because from my limited, young, flesh-and-blood point of view, it seemed they were getting the better end of the deal. Others were on their feet. Others had use of their hands. Others were going to college, holding down jobs, and raising children. To my way of thinking, I was getting the raw end of it all.

But God used a few stern rebukes to get my attention off other people and put my focus back on Him, trusting that He had a purpose and plan and that through Him, I had hope and a great sense of worth. So basically, I dealt with my self-pity by getting my eyes back on Christ.

I don't mean to sound glib or irresponsible by suggesting all this was easy for me—it was not. It took many years for me to finally get a single-mindedness about my faith, because my emotions played such a large part in my early Christian faith, when I was on my feet. If I felt like trusting God one day, I did. If I didn't, I didn't. I was swayed back and forth by fickle feelings.

I believe my injury was God's way of refining my faith so it would rest not so much on my emotions but rather on His character and nature. As I dealt with each of these components of what Dr. Hart calls the "depression spiral," I began to put my loss into the perspective of God's Word and love and purpose and control, and ultimately I got out of the pit of depression.

One of the hardest things to deal with was a sense of claustrophobia, a feeling that it's never going to go away. I would be this way for ever and ever, consumed by the terrible, terrible pain. It was extremely frightening to think it would never pass. What made it so claustrophobic was that I couldn't seem to pull myself out of it. I lay in bed in the hospital, day after day, month after month, for almost two years. Sometimes the calendar seemed to fly by, and at other times to drag, but I was helpless to do anything about it. I remained the same.

It's funny, but the lives of all my friends and family seemed to go on. My friends turned 18, 19, or 20 years old, and it seemed I was forever a 17-year-old for whom time had stood still. Everything was stopped, and I couldn't escape. This claustrophobia and the desperation it created drove me into the pages of Scripture.

I still wrestle with the terrible sense of claustrophobia. It's interesting that I give this testimony while I'm lying flat in bed, where I've been for several weeks, trying to heal a bedsore. I still fight discouragement and depression, because that terrible sense of claustrophobia is intensified when I'm lying down. When I lie down, I have even less movement than when I'm sitting up, because gravity is working against me. Even my voice becomes weak.

Lying here day after day, not being able to read much and having only so much I can do with my time, isn't much fun. So even though books have been written, I speak to a lot of people, and a movie has been made, the paralysis doesn't go away. I have to fight these battles against discouragement and depression over and over. You don't get over them once and for all. God is still using my paralysis to teach me about myself, and through it all He's purging me of bitterness or things that never were adequately healed while I was in the hospital. And the lessons I learned from those severe bouts with depression mean a great deal even now when I have to go through milder bouts.

Looking back on my early battles with depression in the hospital, the most helpful thing my friends and family did was to visit me consistently. That seemed to alleviate the depression. Not sporadic visits here and there a little bit, but if I knew I could count on just one person coming every Friday morning to spend the afternoon with me—perhaps read some Robert Frost poetry to me, do my nails, bring a bag of donuts or a pizza for lunch, bring in a guitar or record albums, or watch a game show with me—it gave me a kind of goal.

On Monday morning, I would start thinking about how on Friday morning my sister Jay would come. I knew that when she came, she would always bring a surprise. Whether it was a different nail color or a new magazine or book I'd heard about but hadn't read yet, she'd surprise me somehow. And I'll tell you, when the week began, what gave me the hope that maybe I could make it through Monday and Tuesday and Wednesday was the knowledge that my sister was going to come in on Friday morning, and we would have fun together.

That's why I think just being there consistently is the best way to minister to one who is either depressed or going through a severe trauma. It doesn't have to be all that often. My sister came just once a week. But it was a time set aside, and I knew she sacrificed other responsibilities and things to come and be with me in the middle of my hurt. And invariably she would bring lots of Kleenex, because she knew I would cry. But I felt safe in her arms, knowing my crying would not drive her away. She'd be there next Friday as I had anticipated.

This idea of ministering in tangible, concrete ways—not always with grocery lists of Bible verses but in regular, realistic ways—wins you the right to be heard so that eventually, when you want to bring some guidance or advice, it will be more readily received because you've proved yourself a friend.

Those who go to people in depression, pat them on the back, and say, "Listen, you've just got to praise the Lord anyway. Put a smile on your face," are really going against Scripture. The Bible says we're to weep with those who weep. You need to get down into the pit with them, put your arm around them, and grieve with them rather than present some pie-in-the-sky ideal that for the moment, at least, you have no realistic way of achieving.

You don't have to have experienced the same trauma to be able to do this, either. Certainly an able-bodied person couldn't walk in here and say, "Gee, Joni, you've been lying in that bed for three weeks with that bedsore. I'm really sorry, and I can understand how you feel." But that person can sit here with me for a while and hold my hand, or maybe just talk or read poetry or something like that. It's so comforting just to know there's somebody who doesn't mind getting down here on this bed with me, so to speak, and spending several hours with me. You don't have to be in a wheelchair to give me that kind of comfort. There are many levels of suffering, and God uses each of us on that scale, no matter where we are, to comfort others at different places on the scale.

Some of you who read this are depressed. You need to realize there are many different kinds of depression and many different reasons people become depressed. Some of it is because of sin. Some has nothing to do with sin. Some of it is because of the chemical makeup of your body. Some of it is simply the Monday morning blues.

I can't speak to depression as a whole, but I can speak about depression that comes as a result of injury, illness, or other negative circumstances. I would encourage you to take the advice of Paul when he said to weep with someone else who can weep with you. You need to grieve, to cry, perhaps even to express your anger to God. As I said earlier, better to get angry at Him than to walk away from Him.

Give yourself time to work through your feelings so you can begin to see your way clearly through the insanity of your pain. Then share yourself with a small, intimate group of friends. Allow them to minister to you in tangible ways. Then, with this group of friends, begin to reconstruct your faith from the pages of Scripture. Let it be your light and guide, and especially your hope and comfort.

You also need to understand that your experiences of suffering are not out of keeping with the Christian life. The Bible makes it clear that when we sign up in the army of Christ, it's going to mean a few bumps and bruises along the way. The writers of the New Testament make it abundantly clear that trials and tribulations are going to figure largely in what it means to grow in the grace and knowledge of the Lord. When we come to Christ, we don't have a guarantee He is going to erase all our pain and problems. He does guarantee He will see us through them and the depression that comes as a natural part of facing them.

This assurance didn't come quickly for me. I remember being shocked at what God was allowing me to go through. I thought, *If God is allowing me to go through all this at such a young age, what in the world is He going to do next?* And I really wrestled with that lack of trust. But I began to see that what I suffered is what the whole human race collectively has to go through. Christians and non-Christians suffer alike. The real difference is that as those who are part of the family of God, we have the assurance that all of this is part of a good plan, a perfect will, a higher mind. But we need to be clear that the cost of discipleship for some will mean the intimate fellowship of suffering.

The greatest thing for anybody who's struggling with depression as a result of injury is that we have hope. We have the assurance that things won't always be this way. We won't always feel this terribly, terribly low. There's a light at the end of the tunnel. Joy does come in the morning after weeping during the night. Ultimately, even in facing a permanent and severe disability or a terminal illness, we have the hope of heaven. We have the assurance that God will make sense out of our most senseless suffering and that one day, there will be a healing of all things. There will be a perfection and glorification of our bodies, and the pain will be wiped away.

For me, the struggles with depression, both in the past and in the present, haven't been easy. But like Job, I want to trust God in the face of my unanswered questions. And I believe, on the basis of His Word, that there is a place and a purpose for my struggles.

E L E V E N

Florence Littauer

Depression occurs in the best of circumstances. Florence Littauer had attained all the goals she had set as a young girl. She developed and sharpened her considerable skills in speech, drama, and English; added the polish of a sophisticated socialite; met and married a highly successful young businessman, from a prestigious family, in a wedding that was covered by Life magazine; and became a moving force in a variety of organizations.

None of those accomplishments filled the emptiness behind the facade of a successful marriage, however. None protected Florence from the emotional devastation that came with having two sons develop a mysterious ailment which, over a few months, changed them from happy, normal babies to ones with no brain activity at all. Her account of how God brought her through the depressions caused by loss, anxiety, guilt, and anger is a testimony to the love and grace of God in the most desperate of emotional circumstances. Her testimony is taken from an interview conducted in May 1980.

From the beginning of my life, I wanted to achieve great things and set goals to accomplish them. Having been brought up in three rooms behind my father's store, where to go from the bedroom to the bathroom you had to pass by the cash register, I felt that somewhere in life there had to be something better for me. I started out very early deciding to make myself into something great. I assumed that if I set goals, I could achieve anything.

In high school, I did all the accepted things to get ahead. I studied hard, joined the right clubs, and was awarded a scholarship to the state university. I went off to become educated and make myself into the kind of person I really wanted to be.

I worked hard in college, where I majored in speech, English, and education and minored in psychology. I studied modeling and drama, read books on etiquette, joined the sorority, ran the parties, became the house president—in short, I did everything possible to develop in me a sense of the social graces. When I got out of college, I felt I was not only totally educated, but a gracious lady as well. I was ready to go!

Where I went was back to my hometown to teach high school, and again, everything I touched was successful. I introduced a speech course and had a large student following (perhaps partly because I was the only teacher under 50). I earned $1,800 my first year and felt I was rich. I thought I had achieved all a poor girl from three rooms behind a store could ever hope to accomplish.

As I gloried in my success, one fear began to creep into my heart, as it would with any single English teacher in the hills of Massachusetts: *What if I never find a man?* One of the problems with having made yourself so wonderful is that there are few men left who are good enough for you, and you don't want to marry downhill. I looked around and found no one in Haverhill I considered worthy of me.

That summer I taught drama at a prestigious girls' camp in the woods of Maine. One evening, as Janice, the sailing counselor, and I were draped seductively over a rock near the local Howard Johnson's looking for some action, a handsome young man came out of the mist. I thought to myself, *This is what you've been waiting for all these years,* and I began to figure out how I could meet him. As I watched, he and his brother came over to Janice, an old college friend, and we all became acquainted. Little did I realize at that time that Fred came from an English Tudor mansion with a maid in uniform and all the things I had always been looking for.

We began to date, courted for a year, and, due to an interesting set of circumstances, were married in a ceremony covered by *Life* magazine. All these events brought me to the ultimate in my status climbing and confirmed the control I had always felt over my life.

But amazingly, when I got married, overnight I became stupid. Fred took me out of my hometown and down to New York, where I was no longer the queen of Haverhill. The hint of things to come came when we returned from our honeymoon. Fred announced that he was now going to put me on a training program. I couldn't believe it! After all, I had trained myself. I knew I was perfect, and for the first time in my life someone was telling me, "You're not perfect. You need improvement." Knowing that my husband felt I needed improvement was a serious blow to my self-esteem and led to a low-level kind of depression, although nothing compared to what would come later.

Materially, our married life went along well. Fred was very successful in his food services business and was in demand as a convention speaker. I found I was married to a man just like me. We were both success oriented. As long as we kept our eyes on the goals, we did all right. When we began to check each other out, we didn't do so well. I didn't do things the way he wanted them done, and I didn't feel I was getting the attention I deserved. So we each began to go our separate ways and developed a level of noninterference with each other. I joined many clubs and organizations and worked my way up to president in a number of them.

I had our first child, Lauren, and then four years later another daughter, Marita. Then finally, to our great relief, we had a son, Frederick Jerome Littauer III. While I didn't really like the confinement of motherhood, I did well at preparing my children to speak correctly, to dress properly, and to behave as model children. I felt it was important that children live on the right side of the tracks, attend the proper school, and take the proper lessons. What I failed to realize, however, was that I did not have the heart of a mother because I didn't know how to love another person. I understood preparation and control, the external and superficial things of life, but I didn't understand love.

When our son was about six or seven months old, he didn't seem to be developing as our daughters had. The people I asked about this would say, "Well, boys are slower than girls. Don't expect him to be the same." But I was increasingly concerned when by eight months of age he couldn't sit up at all, he couldn't seem to hold things well, and he didn't seem to be focusing on me clearly. Then he began to have periods of screaming and crying. Many times in the night when I went to him, he would be rigid, and I couldn't comfort him.

These spasms continued to get worse, and finally, just before he was nine months old, I took him to our pediatrician, who was a personal friend. I handed him over in confidence and said, "Dick, just take care of this child and make him right. Find whatever doctor he needs, do whatever has to be done. Money is no problem."

Dick sent me out of the room and called for a specialist from across the hall. They talked for a while, then brought me back in. Dick said to me, "I think you had better call your husband and have him come down to hear what I have to tell you."

I called Fred, but he was too busy to come. He told me to tell him when he got home. I went back in, and the doctor said to me, "Florence, I'm sorry to have to tell you this alone, but I'm sure this child is brain damaged. I don't know what happened to him, but I'm afraid he's hopeless. I'm afraid you're going to have to put him away and try to forget about him. Perhaps you can have another one."

I didn't cry until I got into the car by myself. On the way home, I looked at my child and thought, *He just can't be hopeless. He is so beautiful. Something must be done for him.*

Fred felt the same way when he heard the news. After all, this was his son. Nothing could be wrong with him.

The next day, the doctor called to tell me he had arranged an appointment for Freddie with a neurosurgeon at Yale New Haven Hospital. This doctor went through a series of tests while we watched. Finally he said, "This child is deaf, blind, and his brain is not functioning. This child has nothing working at all except he is alive. There is really no hope for him."

Both Fred and I were overwhelmed. This doctor said it with assurance. He didn't say "maybe"; he said, "There is nothing you can do for this child." He must have said it ten times, because we didn't want to hear it. We didn't want to believe it. Both of us felt we were super beings. How could we have produced this faulty child? It was a hurt to our pride, to our family, to our background. We tried to refute his statement every way we could, but he patiently stood and waited while we told him why he was wrong. And he ended up saying, "No matter what you say, this child is hopelessly brain damaged." That was the answer.

Instead of binding us together, this tragedy was almost the end of our marriage. It was as if Fred said to me, "Good-bye. I am now going to work more on my business." He got himself involved in everything he could, and he came home as little as possible.

Since Fred "tuned out," I had to tune in. I had to take full responsibility for Freddie. I watched him go from a few to ten or 12 convulsions a day. I had the visiting nurse come in and give him shots that were supposed to control convulsions, but they didn't work. I did everything I possibly could to ease the increasing pain he seemed to be having, but nothing really helped.

I discussed with my obstetrician the possibility of having another child, and he felt it would be the best thing to take my mind off this child. Fred and I also discussed it, and, while he wasn't interested in any more children, he thought it might be the best thing to do to humor me. I did become pregnant, and because I was concerned about the possibility of brain damage, I enrolled in a special program at Yale New Haven Hospital for mothers with brain-damaged children. I was assured that nothing would happen with this one.

During this pregnancy, I had plenty of time to evaluate my life. I sat there holding Freddie as he had convulsions, tears running down my face, wondering where I had gone wrong. How could someone with such good motives and such a positive direction ever get into a situation like this, where everything seemed hopeless? I couldn't figure out how I had ended up with a problem on my hands that I couldn't control.

I had my fourth child, gratefully a son, Laurence Chapman Littauer. While I was in the hospital, Fred, who was always attentive when I was in real need, took Freddie to a private children's hospital. He also decorated the nursery. When I came home, everything to do with Freddie was gone. We were both depressed over our failure at this time, and the only thing we knew to do was to try to forget the bad circumstances that caused the depression. We tried to run away from them or ignore them, and we tried to turn our minds in a new direction. We avoided any mention of Freddie. He was now gone; that was the end of that. I gave my entire attention to this new son.

For the first time in my life, I became a fanatic mother. I guarded Larry. I played with him. I mothered him. I didn't let anybody touch him. This whole experience began to break down the exterior wall I had built, and I started to let out some of the emotions I kept so well hidden. I developed some rapport with my two daughters and got acquainted with them as I never really had before. We became a family—not Fred, just the three children and me.

When Larry was six months old, we got a call from the children's hospital telling us Freddie had died. Fred and I went to the funeral, and I remember the feeling as I looked into the casket and saw this little child who used to be so beautiful. He had little sticks for arms and legs and was bruised where he had hit the sides of his crib in convulsions. Worse than that, he was dressed in what were obviously charity clothes—a little faded outfit. I thought to myself, *This is my son, in second-hand clothes, looking terrible. Couldn't you at least have cared for that child, visited him, done something?* Guilt feelings flooded over me.

I was truly depressed at that time and wondered what good there could be in life. When I got home and saw my daughters, always well behaved and looking so pretty, and my new son who was so bright, I thought that if I could only put

Freddie out of my mind again, I would be all right. So I tried to bury the whole scene and forget the funeral. I went into a cheerfulness act and tried to pick myself up.

One week after Freddie's funeral, I went in to pick up little Larry from his crib and noticed that he didn't seem to respond to me or even hear me. I waved my hand in front of his eyes, and nothing happened. I picked him up and actually shook him as I said, "Don't you do this to me! You have got to be all right!" I had really put my faith for happiness in this new body. I remember clutching him in my arms and driving to the same doctor. I barged right in and said I needed to see Dr. Grainger right away. The minute he saw the look in my eyes, he came running over. He examined Larry, and within a matter of a few minutes he said to me, "Florence, I think it's the same thing."

He arranged for us to take the child to Johns Hopkins six months later in August, and during that time of waiting, Larry went steadily downhill. I watched him go into convulsions, doing the same things his brother had done. I went into deep depression, crying day after day. I felt life was worthless and meaningless. I thought of killing myself. But when August came around, I tried to work up a little hope. Perhaps this new doctor would have some new method, some new thought, some new *something* that would help this child. When I was finally able to talk to the doctor, however, he said, "Well, Mrs. Littauer, I don't have very good news for you."

I asked, "Well, is there any hope?"

He answered, "Come on now, Mrs. Littauer, you know better than that." I knew then that there was no hope.

We took Larry home, his swollen head wrapped in bandages, and after a few weeks his crying and convulsions had all of us in tears. Fred and I took our little Larry to the same hospital where his brother had died just six months before. I remember kissing him good-bye with tears running down my cheeks as I handed him to my husband, who took him inside. I just sat in the car and sobbed and sobbed. That was the last time I ever saw him. They told us he would probably not live to be more than two or three (his brother had died at two), but he is 19 at the time of this interview and is still in that same hospital in Connecticut.

From that point on, my depression was such that I would have tried to kill myself except for the fact that I had those two daughters. Fred didn't matter to me anymore, because he was never around. We just lived together. We never fought. We were both much too refined, too cultured, and too much in control to do that. We were just totally indifferent to each other—emotionally divorced.

I didn't know what to do with my depression. Basically, I wasn't a depressive person. In fact, I was extremely optimistic. As time healed the depression a bit and I was no longer crying day after day, I began to work on controlling the depression by keeping it under wraps. I wanted people to see that I was brave and strong, that I could take it. Friends would say to me, "I don't see how you do it," and that somehow picked me up a bit. It was an artificial stimulus, but it did head me in the right direction. I began to go out and get involved in things, and this activity started to lift my spirits.

It was at this point that my husband's brother Dick and his wife, Ruthie, were listening to a Billy Graham program on television and prayed to ask Christ into their lives. As a result, they began to tell us that maybe we needed some spiritual help. Ruthie kept asking me to a Christian women's club, but I assumed it was probably a group of little old ladies in black dresses with Bibles, trying to be spiritual, and I didn't want anything to do with that. But one day she told me they were holding a fashion show. Now, that appealed to me, and I agreed to go.

To my surprise, the fashion show was beautiful, the music was good, and the decorations were attractive. Then I listened to the speaker, whose name was Roy Gustavson. He told a story of a woman's life that sounded so much like mine that I really thought my sister-in-law had given him advance information. He used Romans 12:1-2 and said that if there were such a lady there that day, she needed to present her body a living sacrifice, holy and acceptable to God, which was her reasonable service. She should not be conformed to the world but be transformed by the renewing of her mind. He said that she would have to turn the control of her life over to the Lord Jesus.

To me, Jesus was some person back in history who told nice parables and was evidently a good man. I wondered how there could be any connection between Him way back there and me right here. The speaker completed the thought by saying, "You may not see any connection, but the Lord Jesus is alive now, and He will change your life. He will do something for you if you are willing to give your life over to Him."

I prayed along with the speaker and asked that I would not be conformed to the world, that Jesus would come into my life and change me, making me what He wanted me to be. Nothing traumatic or unusual happened at that point. I really didn't know what I had done. I didn't know I had become anything. But gradually my attitudes began to change.

I don't want to give the impression that as soon as I received Christ into my life, the depression lifted and I was cheerful again. It didn't happen that quickly. But my conversion experience did affect me and my depression in several ways.

For the first time, I began to realize there was some possible control beyond myself. I already knew I couldn't change my two sons and their circumstances. One was dead, the other was institutionalized, and things were out of my hands. While I had been a "religious" person, I had never heard before that there was a *being* beyond me who could deal with my problems and give me a new perspective.

I don't think I would have been open to this fact previously, because as self-willed and arrogant as I was, I needed to be brought to the bottom before I would look for anything beyond myself to lift me up.

Becoming a believing Christian did not revive my two sons, although that's what I wanted done. It didn't do the impossible, but it did give me the feeling that all was not lost because of this. There was hope in life. I love what Paul says in Philippians 4:11: "I have learned to be content whatever the circumstances." It's such a help to me to realize that while God doesn't necessarily change our circumstances, when we learn to accept them, He moves us on to something better, emotionally and spiritually.

Accepting my circumstances took time. One of the persistent problems was that I always wanted my sons restored, and no one knew how to do that. No matter how I cheered myself by getting involved in things, I would come back home, walk in the door, and be aware that once I had two sons in this house who were no longer there. I could find things to do to keep my mind occupied, and I would even feel quite cheerful. But always, when I returned home and saw my daughters and my house, I knew I had lost two sons. I could never get beyond that depressing realization.

It wasn't until I had some knowledge of the Bible and experience in applying it to my life that I was really able to say, "Lord, You have to take care of this problem. I can't live with this nagging, this concern all the time." As I dealt with this and thought and prayed about it, the Lord gave me peace.

Well-meaning friends had made me feel guilty that I had put Larry in a hospital instead of caring for him at home. I prayed for enlightenment, and soon I was able to accept the fact that I had done what was best for my son. I reassured myself: *He's where he belongs. He doesn't know me. He doesn't need me. He's in a situation that whatever happens, the best care is available. He's in the best place for him.* Only the Lord can rid us of guilt.

The critical point in resolving my depression was deciding I wanted to do something about it. That may sound elementary, but there is a certain comfort in depression. It brings people around us. It brings us attention. It brings us pity from people who want to comfort and care for us. So the turning point for me was when I decided I had better get out of the house, where I had been depressed and crying for months, and get moving and do something. That may have been a human solution, but it works in the spiritual realm as well.

My experience with depression and my counseling of hundreds of others has given me a real appreciation for what friends and relatives can do for depressed people. In my own case, I found they did very little. I don't mean that in a negative way; they were willing to help, but they didn't know what in the world to do with me. They didn't know what to say. Because of that, many friends looked the other way and pretended nothing had happened.

Some of my friends did encourage me to get back in the swing of things. I had to be persuaded to do that. I found it much more comfortable to stay home and be miserable, but they encouraged me to get active again. One friend accompanied me when I went for the various doctors' appointments as we were trying to see our two sons through the various phases. She was the only one to stand by and encourage me.

To those who wish to be of support, I would say: Go and comfort your depressed friend or relative by saying, "I love you, and I am available. I really care, and I will help you." Put your arm around your friend, and hold her hand. Physical contact is very important. It's amazing how people crave a pat on the back, a hand on the shoulder, or just a look of "I care." How often we can help a person by just that much, things I wouldn't have thought of doing before! The Lord has taught me how important love is, and my own experience has shown me the need for compassion for others. Some of the most helpful things we can do are the simplest.

As a friend, you can do these things without having experienced depression yourself. You can say, "I don't understand all you're going through, but I love you, and I want you to know that I will always be here to support you." You can encourage people, listen to their problems, pick them up, and take them out without ever having experienced depression yourself.

If you *have* experienced depression, it will help you understand the depth of despair your friend may be experiencing. Don't be glib with the advice you give. The natural tendency is to tell a depressed person, "Come on, snap out of it," as if that were all there is to it. If you've ever been depressed, you know what that kind of advice can do to you—it just drives you further down. While depression experiences can aid you in being understanding of another, anyone can provide love and support for others who are depressed.

Those experiences of deep depression happened many years ago, but the memories of the feelings of depression, hopelessness, and futility are vivid today. Perhaps that's why the Lord has graciously blessed me with a speaking and counseling ministry to so many depressed people. Through these deep experiences, God has worked the renewing of my being and the healing of my marriage.

Today, Fred and I conduct marriage seminars all over the country. We know we can help, because the principles we teach rescued our own shattered marriage and have proved true over the years since. While I'm not beyond depression today, I have confidence in One who is in control, One who has loved me enough to bring me down to the depths of depression that He might show me my own limitations and His great power.

T W E L V E

Ben Patterson

Ministers experience depression, too. Ben Patterson has been in either full-time or part-time professional ministry for almost 20 years at the time of this writing. Much of that time has been spent in youth ministries, though for some years now he has been a senior pastor. Here Patterson speaks of two major encounters with depression. This testimonial is taken from an interview recorded in January 1981.

My first serious encounter with depression occurred 11 or 12 years ago. At the time, I was area director for Young Life in Riverside, California, the head resident of the men's dorm at Azusa Pacific College, and on retainer with the Forest Home Christian camp as a youth speaker. In addition, I was a full-time seminary student and was also going through a painful breakup with a girl who had been pretty much the focus of my energies up to that point. Further, I was in conflict with the church in which I had grown up and was going through some real changes in my life theologically. I was in tension, overinvolved, and just plain "stretched out."

One night I had a horrible nightmare. I was in a room where ghoulish figures were all clutching at parts of my body. I woke up from the dream really shaken. It was still early, probably about 11:30 P.M., and the sounds of the dorm were all around me, but I had to tell myself, "Hey, look. It's okay. It was just a dream." I was that shaken. When I did get back to sleep, I slept heavily till about 10:00 the next morning, then woke up feeling drugged.

I was used to shaking off my low feelings with physical activity, so I went over to the college track to run for a while. On this particular occasion, the gate to the track was locked. That wasn't unusual; I had often found the gate locked, but I would just climb over the fence and do my running. This time, however, I remember walking up to the gate and looking at it, and the thought of having to climb over the fence to run around the track just seemed impossible. I started to cry.

I thought, *Hey, man, you're in trouble. You've got to deal with this, and you need help.* The fact that I would consider going to a professional counselor indicated how serious I thought the situation was. It was extremely difficult for me to do, because I had always despised that kind of weakness. It was okay for others—I was really patronizing in my attitude—but I could handle my own problems. Seeing a counselor was an admission of failure.

I not only had to admit failure there, but I also quit a lot of what I was doing. I dropped out of seminary, but probably the most painful experience was quitting Young Life. What made this difficult was that I was supposed to be the key man, the one who held it all together. Now I just quit, apparently because I couldn't tough it out. That was hard on me as an ex-jock. I didn't feel free to tell headquarters the real reason for quitting—that if I didn't, I was going to go bonkers. I just told them I was tired, and in my mind that made me a quitter, a bad guy.

My spiritual life dwindled down to the bare essentials during this time. I didn't reject anything, but I more or less said to God that I was not going to deal with certain things between us. I held on to my belief in Him and continued to trust Christ as His Son, but in my life-style, I completely rebelled against the traditional Christian behavior of my upbringing.

During this time of depression and recovery, I think I tried about everything. I drank a lot, I tried a lot of drugs experimentally, and I went through a period of sexual promiscuity. I had always driven a Volkswagen, but I went out and bought a Mustang with a big engine. (After I got married a couple of years later, I spent the first two years of our marriage trying to get down into an affordable insurance bracket because of all the tickets I had received during this time.)

If you had met me before this time, you would have met a responsible young man who really had his act together and was going somewhere. But while I was trying to deal with this huge depression, not able to cope with all the things I was trying to do and getting counseled, I was really a different guy. When I got married, a lot of people looked at my girl, shook their heads, and thought, *That poor girl—she's married a wild man.*

From what I know about depression, my reactions don't seem to be the norm. Rather than retreating into myself and slowing down, I became frenetic in my activity. Far from becoming immobilized, I kept in constant motion. I had a lot of friends and spent a lot of time with them. In fact, I avoided being alone. Whenever I was alone, I felt hopeless, and when I stopped moving, I felt myself spiraling downward. I guess I felt a little like a gyroscope: as long as I was spinning along, I thought I was maintaining my equilibrium. When I slowed down, I thought I was going to tip over.

Two things stand out in my mind as I battled with the depression and began to recover from it. Both were important in my recovery from that traumatic time. First, my counselor was a supportive, nurturing kind of man. Although I had taken enough counseling classes to know what he was doing—the various techniques, voice tone changes, and so forth—I just gave myself over to the counseling. What he did for me more than anything else was to give me permission to not have to be strong. He kept saying it was okay to quit what I was doing, it was okay to fail, it was okay to fall down and cry. I didn't need to be the athlete, the leader, the spiritual whatever I felt I had to be. It was okay to be weak.

The second important thing was the acceptance of my friends. Not all my friends, mind you. With some, the premise of our relationship was the integrity of my Christian life. When that began to wane, so did their friendship. Some of my friends' theology was very liberal, and they had no problem with what I was doing, so I really liked to be with them. Since I've gotten back to my old self in many ways, though, those friends have also dropped away.

But one friend in particular stood by me during this difficult time. He loathed what I was doing, but there was no question that he loved me and was my friend. He was against my drinking and my other activities, but he was for Ben Patterson. When my behavior got me fired from a job, he did his best to find work for me and to make sure I was okay financially. His support was probably the single most helpful thing in my recovery from depression.

My second major encounter with depression occurred about two years ago now. I had what is known as a herniated disk, which was pushing against the sciatic nerve in my back, causing me a great deal of pain. The doctor ordered three weeks of total bed rest, which turned out to be floor rest since the bed wasn't firm enough. I stayed on the floor for three weeks, and then it took another three weeks before I could go back to work.

Nights were the hardest. I'd fall asleep, only to wake up several times during the night. There's something about lying there alone in the dark and cold, and you're in pain. I never realized before how people in pain could get into a really abusive drug dependency. All that stood between me and relief was a little vial of drugs. I would have taken my last pain pill before going to bed, with the next one not due until maybe four in the morning, and I remember many times just watching the clock until it came time for my next pain pill.

I lost control over my emotions, too. On several occasions, friends called me on the phone to see how I was doing, and though I hadn't felt emotional, the moment I put the phone to my ear, I would break down and weep to the extent that I would have to hand the phone back to my wife. I couldn't pull myself together—I was really a basket case.

Several aspects of this illness contributed to my depression. I had used activity to counter my previous depression. I could work out or play some sports. I could get out and do things. But this time I couldn't move. I was stuck in my room, and that in itself was awful. The brutal fact of being immobile, for one who valued his physical strength and athletic ability, was a real downer. Until then, I hadn't realized how much identity, my masculinity, was tied to my physical prowess.

On top of these problems was the guilt I felt as I saw how hard my wife had to work to take care of me. We had two children, one about three and a half, the other about a year old. They were into everything, and the younger one needed to be picked up and handled a lot. Not only could I not help my wife with these chores, but I was an added burden. It just killed me to see how much she was giving when I couldn't give anything back.

Probably the key to my depression, though, was the way this immobilizing back problem reminded me of my own mortality. This was the first real taste of death I'd had. My father had died earlier, but that hadn't affected me the way my own body's deterioration did. I was brought face to face with the fact that the control of the essential things of life, even life itself, was out of my hands.

During this time, the most helpful counsel came from the same friend who had stood by me in my previous depression. He had suffered through a back injury himself and was able to minister to me in a way that no one else did. Many visitors came and left me feeling worn out. This man would spend three or four hours with me, and when he left, I felt as if I'd been given new life.

What he did was to gently put his finger on everything I feared—of being a cripple for the rest of my life, of being an intolerable burden on my family for years to come, and so on. He helped me work through my fear of being at least partially responsible for the condition. Because he had been there, he was able to gently touch all the real sore spots. By bringing them into the light, he really provided healing.

Many other people were involved in easing the depression, too. I can't begin to estimate the value of people who took care of some basic needs. They cleaned the house, brought meals, baby-sat our kids so my wife could go out for a walk on the beach or get her hair cut—things like that.

I must relate one specific event that happened. One morning when I awakened, I couldn't get up and around, and I started weeping and couldn't stop. My wife sat there on the floor with me, comforting me. And apparently while this was going on, some friends knocked on our back door. We didn't hear them, so they went away, but they left a big box of doughnuts with a note attached.

When I got my cry over, my wife went out to get the paper and found the doughnuts. It's crazy, but that was almost as good as the conversation with my friend that I referred to. My world was confined to that bedroom, but here was evidence that something was going on outside. Even in the midst of my tears, someone out there was thinking about me and had left something for me. Simple as that act was, it was powerful medicine to me.

So while my counselor/friend who sat down beside me and got right to my heart was the superstar in my recovery, so to speak, I had this large supporting cast of beautiful people who helped in very practical ways. Both were important through the depression and in my recovery.

The fact that I tend to be a purposeful person both intensified and relieved the depression at turns. On the one hand, I was greatly frustrated and depressed by being unable to carry out many of my plans. On the other hand, though, even when I was down, I started to structure my time. I embarked on a huge reading program, and when that didn't work too well because of my position on the floor, I laid out a plan to become familiar with some classical music (which was a beautiful experience). I always tried to do something, to be going somewhere, even though I couldn't go anywhere. Focusing on these things relieved my depression, although my concentration often wandered.

I came to realize that God was more concerned about what He could teach me through my depression than He was about the way my depression was relieved. While I did learn many spiritual lessons from my depression, I can't point to a spiritual turning point in my recovery. I learned about God and myself from the depression. He really dealt with my pride. He made it clear that I am really a creature. I am not God, and I'm not going to last forever.

I learned to cling to God. I felt a great need for Him, although it took a long time into my illness before I really relaxed and let Him minister to me and teach me.

Besides my personal relationship to God, the most significant learning was in prayer. Through this experience, God released me to long periods of fellowship with Him and to intercessory prayer. Before it had been hard for me to pray for people and for things, because I wanted to get out and *do* it. God began to teach me that through prayer I *was* doing it. That gave me tremendous purpose—I was getting something done. In one conversation with God, I told Him it was too bad I didn't have time to do this when I was well. He said, "You have as much time when you're well as when you're sick. It's the same 24 hours in a day." Today, I'm a much different man in regard to prayer.

One problem I didn't have to deal with was worrying about how God was involved in all of this. I had done a lot of study on the problem of evil, and that was tremendous preparation for my experience with suffering and depression. I never questioned whether God was punishing me or anything like that. I didn't say, "Why me?" In fact, I really felt, "Why not me?" I'm as liable to suffering as anyone else.

But others were wondering about these questions, and I was in the position of having to interpret my illness to them. That was hard, for not only was I down, but I was having to explain to my parishioners, as their pastor, why I was down. I was quite willing to accept that God's hand was right in the middle of my illness, and I was willing to share the lessons I learned.

Beyond that, trying to find the hand of God in my experience in some ultimate sense was a dead end. My first sermon when I got back was entitled "Since You Asked. . ." in response to all the questions I had received. In it I pointed out that I didn't think it did anyone any good to know why you get sick or depressed unless it reveals something in your actions or life-style that contributed to it. Trying to find the reason in some cosmic sense doesn't get you anywhere.

Looking back on my experiences with depression, I can see that I've learned some lessons that will help me to deal more effectively with depression if and when it comes again. I would be willing to let go and let the depression come. I wouldn't try to fight it or ignore it or run away from it. My depression was worst when I tried to fight it off. I think a lot of the emotional problems I've had have been intensified because I was afraid that if I really looked at them and let them come, they would devour me. When I was finally able to accept depression as part of life, it really helped me get over it.

I would also be quicker in yelling for help. I would cling to God and keep open the communication between us. I would ask my church and friends for help in very practical things—housecleaning, baby-sitting, meals. I would not let pride dig us into a hole. In short, I would struggle to have some reference point outside myself. While we often talk about the centrifugal tendencies in people's lives that split them apart, the opposite is just as bad—the tendency to turn everything in. That's depression with a capital *D*. Whether it was the primary force of prayer, the kind acts of friends, or a Beethoven symphony, those external reference points were critical in modifying the centrifugal tendencies of my depression. I would work hard at developing and maintaining them in a future encounter.

Depression is by definition a movement away from growth. For many it is much more—a devastating experience that can mark their lives with uncertainty and fear. I thank God that He has used my depressions to move me in the direction of ultimate growth.

123 adrenalin
stomach disorder

surgeon 107

31

not able to
pray for
themselves
93

passion
through

sense of happiness
56

confidence
85-86

36

34

53